Between Two Worlds

Between Two Worlds

A Psychiatrist and Her Son's Quest for Compassionate Mental Health Care

Ellen L. Bassuk, MD

Daniel M. Schoonover

BLOOMSBURY ACADEMIC
NEW YORK • LONDON • OXFORD • NEW DELHI • SYDNEY

BLOOMSBURY ACADEMIC
Bloomsbury Publishing Inc, 1359 Broadway, New York, NY 10018, USA
Bloomsbury Publishing Plc, 50 Bedford Square, London, WC1B 3DP, UK
Bloomsbury Publishing Ireland, 29 Earlsfort Terrace, Dublin 2, D02 AY28, Ireland

First published in the United States of America 2026

Cover design by Dustin Watson
Cover image © Hulton Fine Art Collection/Print Collector via Getty Images

Library of Congress Cataloging-in-Publication Data is available

ISBN: HB: 979-8-8818-4253-6
ePDF: 979-8-216-27758-3
eBook: 979-8-216-20062-8

Typeset by Deanta Global Publishing Services, Chennai, India
Printed and bound in the United States of America

For product safety related questions contact productsafety@bloomsbury.com.

To find out more about our authors and books visit www.bloomsbury.com
and sign up for our newsletters.

To our treatment team and compassionate caretakers
who understood that schizophrenia is only one part of the complex
human experience.

And to my children for including me in their recovery journeys.

Contents

Illustrations ix
Disclaimer x
Preface xi

Introduction 1

Part I Growing Up in an Unfriendly World 9

1 Mother of a Marginalized Child 11
2 Setting My Moral Compass 17
3 Becoming a Doctor 23
4 The Best Laid Plans 29
5 Where Did My Sister Go? 33
6 How the System Failed Daniel 43
7 "I Didn't Go to School; I Only Went to Timeout" 59

Part II Descent into Psychosis 63

8 Isolated and Lonely 65
9 Boas, Fish, and Bees 77
10 What Did Daniel Have? 83
11 Reign of Terror 99
12 A Community of Spirits 105
13 Florid Psychosis 123
14 Our Broken Mental Health System 129
15 Transforming Psychiatry 141

Part III Journey Back to Personhood 153

16 Tortuous Uphill Road 155
17 The Recovery Process 165
18 Real People, Real Empathy, Real Connection 177
19 Glimmers of Purpose and Hope 183

Acknowledgments 193
References 196
Index 207
Notes on Authors 212

Illustrations

Figures

I.1 Some of the "voices" that comprise Daniel's "community of spirits" who have accompanied him through his journey and still visit him xii
I.2 Diesel xiii
I.3 The Bishop xiv
I.4 The Sheriff xv
12.1 Diesel, the Bishop, and the Sheriff 107
12.2 Diesel 110
12.3 The Fat Man 111
12.4 The Sheriff 112
12.5 Leroy, William, and Ed 114
12.6 The Bishop 116
12.7 The Drill Instructor and Barilla 118

Table

13.1 Daniel's High Point Medical Chart 128

Disclaimer

The authors has made every attempt to provide information that is accurate and complete, but this book is not intended as a substitute for professional advice. This book is not meant to be used, nor should it be used, to diagnose or treat any medical or psychological condition. Furthermore, core events and experiences are true as best as possible to the authors' memory and we have relied on school, medical, and legal records and reports whenever we could. Finally, to protect the privacy of individuals involved, some names and identifying details have been changed.

Preface

Welcome to the Hotel with No Vacancy

I have heard voices since I was nineteen years old. They would harass me all day. They talked nonstop, threatened me if I didn't do what they said, told me what clothes to wear, and the worst—they touched me inappropriately.

I would chew gum, wear bracelets, and bounce tennis balls to try to ignore them. They never stopped. I was like a hotel with no vacancy. I couldn't get them out of my field of vision, and they never gave me a break. It was pure mental torture.

Then in my thirties I got a part-time job at Home Depot for a while, and they backed off. I guess structure and responsibility interfered with them and this gave me hope. It's now five years later and they only interfere from time to time. Some of the voices I like but some are very annoying. Recently with the help of my psychiatrist Dr. Garrett the voices have further receded, and I view them as my "imagination brimming over" or perhaps they are also spirits. This is the first time I've been willing to talk and describe them in detail to other people.

When my son Daniel was nineteen, he smashed the windows of six cars and was charged with multiple felonies that were later expunged. Fortunately, he was hospitalized instead of incarcerated. Less fortunately he was diagnosed with the label I dreaded: schizophrenia. Institutionalized for most of the following year he deteriorated to a point where he could barely function. He was delusional, paranoid, hallucinating. As the voices in his mind grew more vicious and relentless he jammed quarters into his ears, wore a tinfoil-lined hat, and conducted satanic rituals to control them.

> *When people meet or hear about a person who has schizophrenia, they should know they go through torture on a daily basis and be sympathetic.*

To understand his experience in a meaningful and concrete (as opposed to theoretical) way, fifteen years later, when Daniel was willing to describe his perceptions, I hired a graphic designer who, like a police sketch artist, listened to his description of his "community of spirits" and drew what my son saw, heard, and felt. This allowed me to come closer to experiencing what he experienced, to feeling what he felt. The clarity, consistency, and quickness of this process was astonishing, as was Daniel's reaction to welcoming a simple act of acceptance as opposed to diagnosis. It was also the first time that he was willing to share the extent of his voice community in depth with anyone. It made a real difference. He felt more fully seen, validated, and accepted—not a pariah or "psycho" as he usually felt.

Figure I.1 *Some of the "voices" that comprise Daniel's "community of spirits" who have accompanied him through his journey and still visit him.*

> *They're very spirit-like in how they communicate with me...like a manifestation of someone's presence coming from an afterlife. Or a being that hasn't been born of flesh in this world yet. It's either that or it's my brain misfiring. Either way, they're not going to give me the trouble I used to get from them, I don't mind hearing voices at all. In fact, I might even get bored if I didn't have them around these days. Pretty bored.*

Diesel was the first voice to appear. Daniel was living in a residential facility and sitting in the dayroom when she popped into the corner of his vision. He was not startled and thought "*Whatever . . .*" Diesel is a thirty-year-old muscular, bald-headed, large-breasted, attractive woman who is easygoing

Figure I.2 *Diesel.*

and gives the other voices helpful advice like asking them to grill sausages for Daniel. She calls him "Dear" and has been a good friend to him for almost two decades. She never goads him to do strange or destructive things, but might insist that he watch more television, eat two portions for lunch, or go for a long walk. When the other voices are arguing among themselves, Diesel whispers calming words to reduce Daniel's tension. She lives in Hell's Kitchen in New York City and owns a jewelry store that Daniel has visited in his imagination. He likes it when she shows up and misses her if he doesn't see her regularly. She is his companion and special protector.

The Bishop arrived many years later. She is about eight feet tall, looks like Lady Gaga, is pretty, and according to Daniel, "a great voice to have." She wears tall boots, tight leggings, a long jacket, and a winter hat that has a pompom

Figure I.3 *The Bishop.*

on the top—like a bishop on a chessboard. Her most remarkable feature is the monastery located in her chest that includes a little castle that houses ten monks. The monks meditate most of the time and have told Daniel they flew across the ocean to visit him. Bishop may have captured them because she was offended that they were giving away her thoughts, but the monks don't mind because they now have a home. She is fun-loving, goes ice skating, and dances like she is at a discothèque although she always floats—her feet never touch the ground. She is (quite literally) a voice of good cheer and likes Daniel to talk about her *a lot* and gets upset if he doesn't. Daniel finds the Bishop reassuring and just as with Diesel, misses her if she doesn't appear regularly.

The Sheriff is an average sized Native American man who wears big boots and black pants, has long black hair, and lives in an apartment of unknown

Figure I.4 *The Sheriff.*

location. He likes to yell loudly that he is *The Sheriff!* He tries to mediate arguments and keep order among the different voices. Early on the Sheriff threatened Daniel, but over time they became friends. He often says: "I came out of a freezer to be Dan's gentle friend." He is not the leader, but he enforces the rules and protects people.

As you'll see later in this book, many more voices constitute Daniel's community of spirits. Each has a different role—some are kind and cooperative, while others have been malicious and threatening, urging problematic behavior, and trying to kiss or touch him in provocative ways. Others—like Barilla, who is an environmentalist—are more interested in climate change and the state of the world. Each seems to represent some aspect of his personality and experiences. Except for Diesel, the Bishop, and a few others, like my and Daniel's relationship, they continue to evolve and change. They are the backbone of the story we are about to tell. They mirror Daniel's lifelong struggles to grow into an independent adult.

Introduction

Our Mental Health System Is Broken

I have come a long way from the tribulations associated with my mental illness. From the time I was a kid, I was different, excluded, kicked out of school at age eleven, involved with the courts, became suicidal, hospitalized more than ten times, and dealt with as less than human. I lost hope.

With the help of my treatment team, my therapists, and parents, I gradually emerged and have built a new life. I have started to feel like part of the world. I am hopeful.

My volunteer work has given me purpose. Helping people and animals has given me purpose. Some years ago, shortly after my discharge from High Point Hospital when I was twenty years old, I worked at Woods Hole Aquarium, taking care of the large tanks and stranded sea turtles. I've also rescued my current cat, Clara. I chose her because she was the most aggressive cat at the shelter. After lovingly caring for her, she is now docile, cuddly, and devoted. I love seeing her when I walk into my very own apartment. She keeps me company, so I am less lonely.

I am also involved in many activities which give me purpose and optimism about the future. My favorite activities are photography, playing acoustic and electric guitar, martial arts, reiki, and exercising. I also help various disabled and older neighbors.

Although I'm still working on it, I feel I am part of a community of like-minded people. I feel like I am living. Moving into my own apartment at the age of thirty-one was critical in launching this process. It made me feel less powerless and that I now had control over my life. I can make my own choices. I have a life that I want, and people are not dictating everything I do. With all these changes I feel more like a respected, valued person.

I finally feel like I belong somewhere and am accepted rather than being a "psycho."

Our mental health system is broken.

As a psychiatrist, a passionate advocate for families and children who are homeless, and the mother of Daniel who was given the label I always dreaded most—*schizophrenia*—I've come to see that idealism without action is hollow at best. One out of five Americans have a mental health problem, and among those considered seriously mentally ill, more than an estimated 1.5 million have been categorized as schizophrenic and 7 million have been labeled with bipolar disorder (National Alliance on Mental Illness, n.d.); many are grappling with unresponsive caretaking systems. Overall, less than half of Americans with mental health issues receive care, and the average delay in treatment is twelve years (National Alliance on Mental Illness, n.d.). Daniel's and my story illustrates the collapse of critical aspects of health care and the urgent need for an effective, inclusive response from all parts of the system.

This book is a rare, fully documented account of lifelong mental illness told from Daniel's point of view and mine. It spans four decades, beginning when he was six months old, and reveals how, with considerable support from a recovery-oriented team—the core of a holistic system of care characterized by person-centered, strengths-based services where the illness is viewed as only part of a person's experience—Daniel is thriving and continues to grow into a kind, empathic man living a relatively full life, a remarkable shift from a poorly understood, often disorganized, and unrelated boy suffering from serious mental illness with little hope.

From the age of three, Daniel was suspended, expelled, or excluded from almost every school, treatment program, activity, or social event he attended because of his differences, disability, and the associated stigma. Saddled with at least a half dozen diagnoses, many of his providers implemented interventions doomed to failure by their limited understanding of my child, and the ever-increasing rigidity of the medical system. When Daniel was yet again expelled from school at the age of eleven, the Department of Education arranged for an array of skilled consultants to work with him at home. He never again attended school regularly.

Given Daniel's isolation, struggles, and disastrous experiences, I also hired several "case managers" who were not from the mental health system. As a result of what one might call our "do-it-yourself" intervention, staffing, and curriculum creation, we were better able to see Daniel and help him see himself as a boy struggling to grow up who was neither naughty, flawed, nor "a problem." We had no choice; every standard response had failed. The only way to meet my son's unique needs was to create a new blueprint—a recovery-oriented, trauma-informed support system. Our custom-tailored approach was anchored in empowering, respectful, and enduring human relationships, and driven by Daniel's choices, sensitivities, wishes, and hopes about his future. With this in place, my son was at last able to move forward and fashion a life of independence, creativity, curiosity, and accomplishment.

The supports have evolved as Daniel has changed and grown. The most active members continue to be peer providers with "lived experience" who are not blinded by diagnosis and implicit biases about his mental illness. As he became more able to share his inner experience, we added a new psychiatrist to the team.

> *Since 2023 I have been seeing Dr. Garrett, a psychiatrist who has very insightful perspectives as to what the nature of my auditory and visual hallucinations are. . . . He emphatically proclaims they come from my imagination brimming over, and I think he's right. They live within me. I am a hotel with no vacancy. Dr. Garrett. wants me to learn to be the center of it all when it comes to my hallucinations.*
>
> *Although sometimes my hallucinations are the center and not me, I still like sharing the space.*

Daniel's work with Dr. Michael Garrett, Professor Emeritus of Psychiatry at SUNY Downstate Medical Center, was the most recent in a series of events that confirmed my belief that the traditional view of serious mental illness and its use of diagnostic labels is far too limited. The question must be modified from "What is wrong with Daniel?" to "How can we fix the system?" (Or at least avoid the pitfalls.) As Daniel put it, "Random acts of kindness," to which I would add *and humanity,* "are everywhere."

We transformed Daniel's treatment, team into one that was based on Recovery principles. Generally thought of as healing from an illness, Recovery has a different meaning in a systems context. It refers to a "process of change through which individuals improve their health and wellness, live a self-directed life, and strive to reach their full potential" through four supportive dimensions:

- Health
- Home
- Purpose
- Community

The catalyst for this process is hope (Deegan, 1996; Substance Abuse and Mental Health Services Administration, 2014).

The Kraepelinian definition of schizophrenia was formulated in 1899 and continues to influence (and constrict) doctors and mental health providers (Rybakowski, 2019). This belief that schizophrenia is an inevitably deteriorating illness with no hope of remediation is gradually being supplanted by the knowledge that healing is possible and that many people can lead fulfilling, or at the very least, better lives and become valued members of the community (Meyers, 2010). Symptoms are but a small part of the experience and can be managed through treatment, medication, and dedicated care. Even with serious mental illness, people can be "in recovery," engaged in a personal and self-directed journey buttressed by a community of supporters including peers. Instead of being illness-centered and deficit-oriented, this process is person-centered, and illness is only one part of each human's experience (Davidson, 2016). Recovery promotes growth and is a lifelong process of discovery. As Patricia Deegan, a psychologist and disability rights advocate, wrote: "Recovery has its seasons, its time of downward growth into the darkness to secure new roots and then the times of breaking out into the sunlight. But most of all recovery is a slow, deliberate process that occurs by poking through one little grain of sand at a time" (Deegan, 1996). Daniel's experience supports this.

As Daniel traveled his Recovery path, he was increasingly able and willing to share his inner experiences and perceptions. When he was in his mid-thirties, we began to discuss the lost years of his childhood, his voices or "community of spirits," and some of the other challenges, mistreatment, and even abuse he endured. He became increasingly engaged and interested in talking about how he has struggled to regain his personhood and chart a path to a purposeful life despite the myriad diagnoses including ADHD, OCD, Tourette syndrome, temporal lobe epilepsy, his tumultuous adolescence punctuated by a psychotic break, and his many, *many* schools, therapists, doctors, experts, and hospitalizations. As he became more confident, he was eager to share his experiences from his childhood and feel affirmed and known by others. He wanted people to hear his story and benefit from what he endured.

Our discussions were at times excruciating and sad but led to a revisiting and better understanding of the feelings associated with Daniel's years of chaos, uncertainty, sorrow, and suffering. Even more importantly, these conversations in their own way became part of his treatment plan, contributing to his increasing growth and wellness and his intense wish to have people bear witness to the devastation of his illness, various system challenges, and the strategies he used to help him in the recovery process. Because of these exchanges as he welcomed me and others into his alternative reality, we decided to write this book. This decision simultaneously strengthened our relationship and his increasing independence from me. This was the power of feeling valued and validated, as an equal and active member of the world.

Sometimes our conversations dredged up memories that he, I, and sometimes both of us had suppressed. Rereading hundreds of pages of psychological and medical records and school evaluations, talking to case managers, and reviewing the relevant literature gave me the opportunity to create a sequential, meaningful narrative of what happened to us and our family as a result of Daniel's illness. At times, the process was painful, filled with grief and sorrow for the missed opportunities, the horrific episodes, a deeper understanding of Daniel's experiences only in hindsight, and lament for the decades Daniel lost.

These conversations also highlighted the unfulfilled possibilities that most parents harbor and heightened concerns about the future. But side by side with these feelings arose ones of accomplishment and at times joy focused on who Daniel has become, the challenges we surmounted, and a renewed hope about his future. Most of all, Daniel is now an independent young man who is sweet and kind, has many unusual talents and interests, a real capacity for empathy and connection to animals and people around him, and an intuitive compassion for those less fortunate. He is continuously working to manage his symptoms, live with his voices, and accept that they are part of him, reflecting aspects of who he is. Most importantly, he has learned that he is not his illness. Daniel is Daniel. He still hears and sees voices, but they no longer control him, and he relates to them differently.

As I write this, Daniel is forty years old and our story of mother and son, of advocate and patient, coincides with the striking changes in the healthcare system and the increasing challenges in the treatment of people with serious mental illness. In doing so, it is important to underscore that our understanding of how the brain works—or as Daniel describes it, "misfires"—is still in its infancy and will undoubtedly add to our toolbox of effective interventions as we learn more. I believe that many of Daniel's difficulties reflect the stigma about serious mental illness, the role of traumatic stresses, environmental determinants, and the limitations in our healthcare system that contributed to his decline. When our medical, educational, and criminal justice systems are ready to acknowledge and embrace the transformative potential of personal empowerment and human connections and have successfully advocated for sufficient resources, my son's ultimate success will become the norm as will that of many, many others.

Over the decades I have been a psychiatrist, I have experienced these challenges firsthand—especially the transformation of healthcare into big business; I have lamented its deterioration. Revenue and profits continue to grow at extraordinary rates. Some of these challenges are reflected in overcrowded emergency rooms, understaffing, long waiting lists, accelerated patient visits, insufficient bed capacity, and difficulties with insurance reimbursement (Barish, 2012). Furthermore, health disparities loom large, compromising the ability of many people to access healthcare. These limitations raise critical questions about how we can refuel healthcare and mental health care. They especially raise questions about psychiatry and how we can reverse the growing focus on fifteen-minute medication appointments back to its base as a psychotherapeutic relationship between doctor and patient, where medication is prescribed as necessary, and the doctors share their expertise with other providers.

I am fully aware that if my family hadn't had resources, little of this would have been possible. I have learned that what matters most when it comes to mental illness and recovery is reliable, empathic, nonjudgmental care aligned with an individual and combined with an open-minded perspective—seeing beyond labels, differences, symptoms, and diagnoses. One that is both empowering and non-stigmatizing. With single-minded focus, it is possible (although difficult) for people to seek out and find humane treatment, but the resources are exceedingly limited. It takes a lot of work. Our unrelenting attention ultimately allowed Daniel to compose a life with purpose, meaning, and some joy, and it is our earnest hope that our insights will help others do the same regardless of circumstances.

Daniel and I share a dream for this book to be the next chapter in advocacy: our story illustrates the urgency of creating and implementing a new vision of person-centered compassionate care that individuates rather than systematizes and is integrated into a healthcare system that echoes this transformation. It is a cautionary tale of how families and individuals who are different must step out of traditional models and seek and even fight for humane approaches that view illness as a single element of a person's whole experience and recognize and affirm the totality of their life and hopes—the heart of the Recovery movement. We strongly believe Recovery-oriented trauma-informed strategies can support people with differences, and that there are caretakers who are reliable, consistent, compassionate, and devoted who can help people like Daniel thrive. We hope others will travel with us on this continuing journey.

Part I

Growing Up in an Unfriendly World

1

Mother of a Marginalized Child

As an enthusiastic new mother, I took young Daniel to a Gymboree program. While the other children were lined up in a row, Daniel was mesmerized by the record player. Instead of running across the room when the teacher signaled, Daniel remained transfixed by the spinning turntable.

The seeds of Daniel's otherness were sown early during infancy—I realized as both a doctor and a mother that his growth and development were unusual from the beginning. I intuitively knew we were on our own path and had no choice but to travel it. Unique and vulnerable, my role was to love and protect him and make him as safe as possible in a world that doesn't easily accept divergence. I did my best to remain an unrelenting advocate, a critical role that is challenging at best and often impossible for parents to fulfill.

Raising a son with Daniel's extreme difficulties and unusual strengths meant traveling a road of loss, grief, and chronic sorrow, intermixed with hope and joy. I love him for all his challenges and quirkiness, his sweetness in the face of adversity and exclusion, and for his unusual talents. I love him because he is my son, and he has overcome so much with such grace. He has reached the other side of many of these experiences and continues to grow and embrace his inherent humanity. His otherness opened a world that went well beyond the constriction and boundaries of the traditional one I had lived in. It revealed a realm of spirits, an appreciation of the vulnerabilities of others like himself, and the uniqueness of each of us and even nature. Daniel taught me what diversity and difference really mean, helping to transform me into a more open, flexible, and loving person who can better see and embrace the commonality and exceptionality of each of us.

These lessons were not without considerable sadness for Daniel and our family. Even now, as an older parent, I grieve for the decades of his life dominated by mental illness and for the ways he was treated, excluded, and changed—no child should have to experience this. Unlike traditional grief in which there is a definitive loss, a child's serious mental illness means letting go of hopes and dreams for what might have been. There are few rituals or supports that help acknowledge this, making the journey lonely at times. Sometimes referred to as "disenfranchised grief," it is an ambiguous loss without the usual supports or acknowledgments that accompany other losses (Smith, 2022). There are no rituals to mitigate this type of pain. Instead, it means giving up faith in the benevolence of the system and dealing with its inadequacies, usually alone, which in Daniel's case often made his life unbearable, and missed or even ignored the humanity of each of us. As his mom, it was heart-wrenching to be relatively powerless to prevent or lessen his suffering. Even now as an adult, he continues to deal with the painful feelings that he endured as a child.

I have asked myself many times how we survived the heartaches of his life, and how as his mother I retained an optimism and belief that he would grow up and thrive in his own way. Even when I did not know how, the answer was "Yes" because he was my son and I had faith in him, and how with persistence and unrelenting dedication he would turn out to be okay, just different. I came to appreciate that situations often got better when I bypassed the biases in the traditional healthcare system and moved ahead in directions tailored to Daniel's needs. This often meant taking a nontraditional path.

There is little question that my career as an academic psychiatrist and activist deeply involved with children experiencing homelessness and trauma was in many ways advantageous. It helped put our experience in a long-term perspective after working with families in shelters. I met many moms experiencing homelessness who were relentless advocates for their children and were successful in surmounting many obstacles. They did not succumb to the vagaries of the "non-system" of care. Still, others struggled, and their children suffered as a result.

At times during Daniel's childhood, I functioned in full "coping mode" almost on autopilot, but always with an underlying tension and dread as I anticipated the next crisis. I often wondered whether I could do better as a mother and if I was up to the challenge. These worries were intensified by the many doctors, educators, social workers, and police who readily blamed me for Daniel's problems. The special education school personnel insisted I was too enmeshed with my son and should spend less time with him; I wondered how they could be so blind to his needs. The detectives who charged him with various crimes aggressively blamed me for negligence and his "bad behavior." The therapists we saw countered their accusations; instead, they told me I worried *too* much and was *too* anxious. We worked on ways to reduce my stress and manage my guilt, which they emphasized was largely unfounded. Even my father at times wondered why I had such a poorly behaved child. *Couldn't I do better?* Sometimes I wondered if Daniel had been adopted by another family, would things have turned out differently? Over time and with more therapy and experience, I was increasingly able to moderate my worries and acknowledge that I am a worrier about most things. I also knew that I was doing the absolute best I could for my son.

Despite a culture that blames parents overall (Smith, 2022), I weathered this experience, and it has made me a more complete but weary person. My uncommon perspective as a parent and mental health professional allowed me to step back and use my clinical training to keep my feelings in check and maintain a vision of Daniel's future, with him thriving and happy, and to fully accept his unique journey no matter how different it was. (Tsabary, 2010). At times it helped me deny the severity of our situation, but it led to my increasing disillusionment with the systems that, as a young medical student, I had looked to as a beacon.

Sometimes, late at night when I had trouble sleeping (which was often), I mulled over the various individual and systemic challenges we faced, trying to figure out strategies to improve things for Daniel and our family. These challenges were numerous and ultimately fell back on the shortcomings of the system. I knew that being a parent of a child who is so different is not without considerable cost. It requires constant work, energy, and vigilance, not to mention money. Advocating for Daniel was often a full-time job. I was almost always anxious about the future and made plans when he was a young child for the possibility that he might never become fully independent. Fortunately, even when I became a single mom, I had resources that made the course easier. I also knew (and authored some of) the research literature about people living in poverty, how those of different racial and ethnic backgrounds or who are different have worse long-term health outcomes in comparison to their more societally and financially advantaged counterparts (Bassuk et al., 1996; Bassuk et al., 1997; Bassuk et al., 2015). I also knew that as a society, seriously mentally ill people are stigmatized and relatively neglected. However, as the Institute of Medicine report, *Crossing the Quality Chasm*, convincingly describes: "Health care is plagued today by a serious quality gap" that affects most consumers regardless of resources (Institute of Medicine Committee on Quality of Health Care in America, 2001).

Shame associated with mental illness makes the parenting of a marginalized child even more challenging. Mental illness is widely stigmatized in our society both by individuals and systems, undermining compassionate care and making it more difficult for families to access and negotiate comprehensive treatment. As Erving Goffman described in his 1963 landmark book *Stigma: Notes on the Management of Spoiled Identity*, stigma refers to society's perception of "undesired differentness" that marks people as "other" (Goffman, 1963). According to Ashley L. Peterson, in *A Brief History of Stigma*, Othering (which she capitalizes intentionally), "is more than a recognition of differences; it's a judgment about the meaning of those differences that has profound implications for those who are Othered" (Peterson, 2021). Perceptions of mental illness are associated with socially learned stereotypes and the discriminatory behavior that follows. Implicit biases abound and must be addressed, especially among providers.

Reflecting attempts to reduce the stigma associated with mental illness is the ongoing debate about how to refer to it: *mental illness, mental health, mental disorders, mental health conditions, or behavioral disorders?* There is little agreement even about the use of first-person language. Regardless of how it is labeled, the symptoms of serious mental illness have helped mark Daniel as Other or, as he would describe it, "psycho and freak," rather than a person with a not uncommon illness that is only a small part of his experience and humanness.

Because we didn't fit into the fabric of "normal" families, we had to create our own unique support system, which became the mainstay of Daniel's recovery. Even within my extended family, there was limited understanding of the enormity of his problems and their impact on his sibling, father, and me. They had their own children and pressures and were generally distant and unavailable. We had little community support; neighborhood children and their parents often shunned us and had various biases about Daniel's difficulties. He was not a kid who was invited to birthday parties, included in playdates, or asked to join a team. He was bullied, ostracized, and blamed for his outrageous behaviors—if a streetlight was out on our block, we invariably got a call accusing Daniel.

Explanations didn't matter; our lives and futures were too different. I often felt as lonely and sad as Daniel, but it didn't start out that way.

2

Setting My Moral Compass

My childhood home in Jamaica Queens was a brick colonial with three bedrooms on the service road of a six-lane highway between Manhattan and both New York airports. Cars were lined up and down the streets, and dogs wandered freely. We had a small backyard, a few peace roses carefully tended by my mother, and a straggly grapevine. The centerpiece was a gnarly peach tree that split right down the middle after a hurricane when I was about eight years old. I remember that storm—huddling with my three sisters in front of the fireplace in the dark, frightened by the eerie shadows and the slow crack of the tree trunk.

I've come to see how, like that resilient peach tree, my values are deep-rooted in my family's Eastern European Jewish heritage. Before they came to America, my grandparents lived under Russian domination in the Pale of Settlement, a western region of the Russian Empire which from 1791 to 1917 included much of Ukraine where almost all of my relatives came from,[1] the entirety of modern-day Belarus, Lithuania, Moldavia, and east-central Poland, small parts of Latvia, and what is now the Russian Federation. The Pale was one of the few places Jews were allowed to live—at its peak, the population exceeded five million. Jews were not permitted to own land and relied on small service or artisan work to survive. However, Jewish culture and education blossomed in

---

[1]Author's note: My paternal grandmother came from Romania.

the small towns called *shtetls* and led to the flourishing of the modern yeshiva system and the primary focus on education anchored by Judaism ("Pale of Settlement," 2025; Howe, 1976).

The Jews living in the Pale were desperately poor. To meet the needs of the population and in the tradition of *tzedakah* (charity), a volunteer network of social welfare organizations was developed supplying things like medicine, education to orphans, and kosher food to soldiers. By the end of the nineteenth century, one in three Jews in the Pale was supported by these organizations. This was consistent with the notion of *Tikkun Olam*, which in Hebrew means "repairing the world." It is the Jewish mandate dictating social justice—responsibility for humanity through good deeds and social activism. "Jews bear responsibility not only for their own moral, spiritual, and material welfare but for the welfare of society at large" (Shatz et al., 1997).

Living in the Pale meant living in an economically bleak world, with little opportunity, despised by the Russians, surrounded by the constant threat of their anti-Jewish pogroms that obliterated whole communities, and the certainty that male children were destined for conscription into the Red Army at the age of sixteen to face torture and brutalization because of their religion. As a result, many residents fled. According to Irving Howe, in *World of Our Fathers*, "in the thirty-three years between the assassination of Czar Alexander II and the outbreak of the First World War, approximately one third of European Jews left their homelands—a migration comparable in modern Jewish history only to the flight from the Spanish Inquisition" (Howe, 1976).

My paternal grandfather was among these refugees fleeing in 1898. My dad's family immigrated to America roughly a generation before my mother's and was able to establish a successful business. The oldest of five brothers, Dad became a New York real estate lawyer and housing developer, always properly dressed in a suit and tie, even-tempered, intellectual, and emotionally remote. The stresses of his family's escaping their homeland and migrating across the ocean to an unknown future were rooted in a historical trauma from which multiple generations have grown. Yet spirit and faith, planted on a foundation of Jewish beliefs, made the journey and transplanting easier, or at least meaningful, allowing for the possibility of hope.

No wonder then that my childhood home was driven by honoring family, my father's conviction that "blood is thicker than water," and his commitment to Jewish rituals. As a patriarchal liberal Jewish man, he quietly dictated the structure of the household. He was observant, which meant he went to synagogue regularly and honored myriad Jewish holidays. My sisters and I attended Hebrew school three times a week, and we all had Bat Mitzvahs. My father determined the rules, which my sisters, mother, and I followed without open dissent: weekly piano and tennis lessons, and excellence at school. We were kept busy. If I got a 96 percent on a test, he would ask how many classmates did better. Nothing ever seemed good enough. Consistent with his Jewish values, we ate kosher meals together every night, although I refused at a young age to eat meat since it was washed, salted multiple times, and tasted more like leather than food, so my mother indulged me and prepared spaghetti with Velveeta cheese to avoid conflict.

My father was devoted to his family. I remember his exuberance bringing home surprises for all of us—fruit pies and brown licorice that we all loved from the Lower East Side. He and I went on outings together because we shared an interest in collecting stamps. These were special times for me. However, as I became an adolescent, our conflicts went beyond spaghetti. When I found out he had evicted a tenant from one of his apartments, I stormed into his office to confront him with what I viewed as his hypocrisy. His secretary threw me out.

My father made no secret of how much he adored my mother. She was the youngest of five siblings—she and her sister were born in America. My maternal grandparents and three uncles left the Pale (Ukraine) in 1906, arriving through Ellis Island. My grandparents stayed with their *landsman* (countrymen) ghettoized in a humble neighborhood in Brooklyn, never adapting to American culture. Not once did I have a direct conversation with my grandmother, who only spoke Yiddish. Despite growing up in abject poverty with parents who didn't speak English and never assimilated, Mom graduated from high school, became a dental hygienist, married my successful father, and made a half-hearted attempt at college but dropped out to care for her young family.

On Saturday nights, my parents would dress up—always looking glamorous as they drove to Manhattan to attend a play or concert. My father lavished my mom with fur coats and expensive jewelry she would have never bought for herself, because at her core she was the poor kid from Crown Heights, Brooklyn. Although she shopped for herself at department stores like Loehmann's and Macy's, looking for bargains, a few times a year, Mom would take my older sister Carol and me shopping in the fancy Fifth Avenue stores. I looked forward to these trips and planned the clothes I wanted to be cool and stylish. Although down-to-earth and warm, my mother was tough on us about our appearance, perhaps because my grandfather was a tailor, and she wanted to improve upon his circumstances. He died suddenly before I was four years old, so I never got to know him. Mom insisted we dress "properly" for school, wearing bobby socks, slips underneath pleated skirts, and blouses that were starched and ironed. I felt like I never looked exactly right.

Typical of many poor families, my maternal grandparents chose one sibling—my mom's brother Bill—to receive the bulk of their limited resources. He became a wealthy dentist who drove a Lincoln Town Car and ignored his brothers who were struggling manual laborers. Bill seemed sophisticated—smoked and drank at night, was a history buff, and gave me a glimpse of a worldly life to which I aspired. He lived near us in Queens and adored my mom, whom he spoke with several times a day and saw at least once a week. He had been a soldier in the Second World War on the Anzio beachhead, which further romanticized him for me. He forbade buying anything German, was opinionated and intolerant, and made sure reminders of the war were not present in our lives. Despite his prohibitions, the legacy of the Holocaust was somehow transmitted to all of us and became a lens through which we saw the world. The treatment of our ancestors in the Pale of Settlement (mainly Ukraine), followed by the First and Second World War, and especially the horrors of the Holocaust, stories of their emigration, and growing antisemitism worldwide created an unassailable intergenerational trauma that is entrenched in our consciousness.

My mother and her sister were the only members of her family (five siblings and parents) who were born in the US. She was a warm, energetic person. Except for my mother's occasional frustrated outbursts that I had trouble taking seriously and somehow knew were not about us kids, she was a creative person tethered to her daughters and my father, but as with many wives in the early 1960s, she had few outlets except photography and painting. After high school, she became a dental hygienist. She was the extrovert and social director in our family and very much "one of the girls." We spent a lot of time together, doing puzzles, playing games, especially Monopoly and Scrabble, and after school, I usually told her everything that went on during my day. We talked primarily about events, not the feelings underlying them. Along the way, I came to understand she needed me to make her feel whole.

On the surface, my childhood home was idyllic, friendly, and harmonious, but tensions and conflicts seethed underneath. Even now, decades later, conflicts persist but remain unnamed. The family style was to never acknowledge or talk about serious concerns, like when our neighborhood was rezoned in an attempt to integrate some of the high schools. I was sent to another part of Queens—far away from my home, friends, and my sisters. I had no choice. I begged my father to put me in private school anywhere, but he told me this experience would be character-building—a conversation that infuriated me, but he repeatedly ignored my distress despite my persistence.

I dreaded going to high school every morning, refused to eat breakfast, and plaintively complained to my mom that I didn't feel well, hoping she would let me stay home. She ignored me and instead would send me back upstairs to put on a slip or to fix my long red hair. Together we'd sit at the dining room table watching for the bus to come down the hill and make the turn onto the service road in front of our house. I would hurriedly say goodbye and reluctantly begin the trek to school—first a bus ride that passed through a bustling, crowded shopping area that was filled with retail stores, then onto an elevated train, and finally a long walk to Richmond Hill High School—with no green lawn, schoolyard, or athletic fields or teams—surrounded by cement, apartment buildings, and traffic.

I felt out of place and stood out; most of the girls seemed sophisticated, interested in boys and motorcycles, and were dressed in stylishly provocative clothes; academics didn't seem to matter. Out of a graduating class of six hundred, only forty went to college. My clothes, hair, freckles, and good grades classified me as a nerd. I was also younger than the other kids because I had skipped a few grades. However, my advocacy days began early in high school when three of us nerds founded *The Scimitar,* a newspaper addressing the shortcomings of Richmond Hill High and almost getting suspended.

It was these sorts of things I'd share with my mother when I came home after school. I would take a deep breath, change into my blue jeans and sweatshirt, and head to the basement where I'd often find her in the laundry room ironing the sheets with a mangler and escaping the household bustle. Although she channeled her frustrations into her creative interests, it seemed to me that she lived through her daughters' accomplishments. She was exceptionally supportive of our successes and helped steer my two younger sisters toward crafts, painting, and textile arts like quilting, although that wasn't the route for me. When I was growing up, I wanted to become a lawyer like my father, and then a judge, but I unwittingly followed my older sister Carol on a path I would walk for my entire life.

3

Becoming a Doctor

When a friend of my parents suggested I babysit for a preteen girl diagnosed with schizophrenia, I was excited about my first job, but these feelings were tempered as time passed. I was fifteen years old, and she was a few years younger, but she had been in and out of Creedmoor Hospital, one of the enormous inhumane warehouses for people with mental illness in Queens. She was uncommunicative, moved strangely, and frightened me because I couldn't figure out how to engage her. This experience, combined with my parents' involvement with and positions on the Board of Trustees of Lifeline Center for Child Development, one of the first New York day schools that offered "highly individualized, quality educational, therapeutic, and wellness services for children with special needs and other developmental challenges" (Lifeline Center for Child Development, 2021)—mainly children with autism—sparked my lifelong interest in mental illness, the stigma associated with it, and my concerns about its archaic treatments.

From an early age, the question was planted in my mind: Why were people separated, othered, and institutionalized for being different? My education and career brought answers, but ultimately more questions.

I attended Brandeis University, the same college as my sister Carol, and by the time I was nineteen years old, I ended up at the same medical school—we were two of only four women in our class of 110 at Tufts University School of Medicine. Today, over 50 percent of medical students in the United States are women (Murphy, 2021). I was also much younger than everyone else, so it was natural for Carol to distance herself from me, her little sister, but despite her best efforts, we were thrust together. Everything was alphabetical, so we even shared a dissection cadaver. Although we were together during the day, we lived on separate sides of the city—she in Chinatown and me in Cambridge with my college friends.

During our medical school graduation in 1968, my mother became acutely ill with severe and unexplained chest pain, was airlifted to New York City, and admitted to Sloan Kettering Memorial Hospital. She was given a dire diagnosis of reticulum cell sarcoma, which turned out not to be the case. The doctors then assumed she had breast cancer that had spread to a lung and performed a thoracotomy. Just after the operation, a doctor met with Carol, Dad, and me to tell us Mom had six weeks to live and should get her affairs in order. Unable to console a shocked and grieving family, the doctor transmitted this catastrophic message in a robotic manner, as if reading from a script. My father was shattered and could only ask, "Is there no hope?" The doctor definitively pronounced "No."

My medical internship was scheduled to begin in a few days, and I was shaken by this unexpected and devastating information, but when I saw my mom that afternoon, despite the tubes everywhere, she reassured me she was not going to die until all four daughters were married. I wanted to believe her and reminded her of my dream of having two children of my own. From that time onward, for the next fourteen years, her illness became both the backdrop and focus of my life. She was gutsy and resilient—jokingly calling her oncologist "Dr. Undertaker." She returned to a relatively normal life after almost a year of hospitalization. She embroidered the Serenity Prayer and hung it up in our kitchen and chose to live by it. She traveled around the globe with my father despite her episodes of severe illness requiring hospitalization. Her courageous attitude and will to live later made her a favorite at the hospital but also highlighted the challenges of accurately understanding because she ultimately turned out to have multiple myeloma, which is a bone marrow cancer affecting a type of white blood cell production, and in those days was relatively untreatable.

My mother's illness interrupted the natural maturation of our relationship into an adult one. I was still her kid, unconsciously given the task of making her feel whole. I became the designated family spokesperson, relaying any bad news—and there was always a plethora of that. It was an unenviable position, and I resented my father for putting me in it. He was passive and sad all the time. It was only later that I understood how deeply he was grieving and struggling with issues related to illness and death. My sisters and I worried whether my father would survive if something happened to Mom.

Because I didn't know how much time we had, I spoke with my mother almost daily and frequently flew from Boston to New York during my medical-surgical internship at Mount Auburn Hospital in Cambridge, Massachusetts. In a strange way, my intense involvement with work was a relief.

When I became a resident, I was intrigued by emergency medicine because of the immediacy and focus on "fixing" someone. Boston City Hospital had all the drama and excitement of a television soap opera. I thought I would become a surgeon, but I rapidly came to my senses as I saw the long hours and complete commitment that were necessary, as well as the specialty's general lack of interpersonal contact with patients. Surgeons in the ER were healers and saved lives, especially in a trauma unit, and I held these colleagues in great esteem, yet it seemed in ways they were like plumbers. Plus, this was in the early 1970s, and sexism pervaded every aspect of medicine, especially surgery. As a woman, I was often tapped to do the "scut work," and the hierarchy was immutable. These things, combined with my dreams of having a family of my own, led me to reconsider.

As an idealistic kid who grew up in a protected middle-class environment in which helping other people was a central value, I chose the relatively new specialty of psychiatry. In the 1970s, this seemed the best option—interested in the body and mind, focused on developing healing relationships, and helping people live productive lives. I believed it was where humanistic, compassionate care dominated, and as my father had taught his daughters, health and racial equity mattered. As a critical medical specialty for so many people, psychiatrists had specialized training and expertise based largely in the patient-physician relationship. However, in the years that followed, as psychiatry became more "scientific" and weighted toward medications and understanding brain function rather than holistic patient care, I gradually became less enamored.

During my second year of residency, at twenty-five years of age, I was farmed out to Boston State Hospital (which has since been razed) and given the daunting responsibility of running a large catchment area inpatient unit of people with serious mental illnesses who lived in extreme poverty and deprivation. The unit was terrifying; the care was custodial and focused on control, not treatment. Medications and seclusion rooms were relied upon to subdue patients and ensure everybody's protection. The hospital was poorly staffed with few resources, so our job was to ensure safety and prevent bedlam. During this time, I became a proficient psychopharmacologist, doling out medicine to treat—but most often to sedate and subdue—patients.

I awakened each morning with a pit in my stomach. When I arrived at work, my first questions were about whether any fires had been set, fights broken up, weapons found, or people injured. My next concern was whether the people in seclusion rooms had safely been fed. During my workday, I feared for my well-being and gingerly crept around checking to safeguard that no patients were in the hospital's secluded stairwells. I became hypervigilant—always aware of who was behind and in front of me. I was assaulted three times that year—nothing severe enough to require major medical care, but most certainly increasing my dread. The entire experience solidified my identification with the underdog, and along with several of my colleagues, I became a fierce advocate for the patients we so poorly cared for.

We were not only short-staffed, but the building was decaying and there were minimal funds for repairs. The stalls in the women's bathroom did not have doors. The sleeping quarters were dormitory-like, and there were few private spaces. When a colleague was shot and killed on the unit across the hall from me, there was little doubt that it was only a matter of time before the hospital would be closed, which converged with the era of deinstitutionalization and a half-hearted shift of care to the community.

During my third year of residency, I was reassigned to a sheltered, resource-rich academic teaching hospital: Harvard's Beth Israel, which had a small inpatient unit, double and private rooms, more-than-adequate staffing, and many eminent psychiatrists on staff. What a difference! I was also one of the few people who had extensive experience medicating severely ill patients and wrote a psychopharmacology textbook with my colleagues during that time.

All the while, I was learning from my supervisors and mentors about how to become a skilled psychotherapist and quickly built up a clinical practice treating patients with a wide array of psychiatric disorders. Psychodynamic psychotherapy—the interplay of the unconscious and conscious mental and emotional forces that determine personality and motivation—became my gospel and the lens through which I viewed my relationships and the world. I was a sponge, soaking up this knowledge and using it to better understand my own anxieties, fears, and family.

I questioned little during those early days. As a young female physician specializing in psychiatry, I naively and almost blindly trusted in the wisdom, ideals, and altruism of the field and its person-centered approach. The first crack in my devotion to this worldview occurred around the decision about whether to enter formal psychoanalytic training. I had an unfamiliar resistance to going ahead with it—and finally attributed it to my earlier work with poor and deprived people who experienced so much adversity, had limited access to mental health care, and ended up in horrendous settings like Boston State Hospital. Psychoanalysis was largely for the "worried well" who had time and money. Although this perspective is somewhat facile, it was the kernel of my decision not to go ahead with formal analytic training, and instead be sure I could treat multiple patients, many of whom were poor people of color and traumatized, and at the same time continue my advocacy activities.

Over these early years, I came to see that even psychiatry was not addressing the pressing questions related to mental illness, especially the effective treatment of serious mental illness, the nature of Recovery, the role of psychosocial stressors and trauma, and the impact of poverty, racism, sexism, and culture. This led me to become dispirited by its transformation into a business driven by medical technology in which psychiatrists seem to have forgotten that we indeed know little about how the brain functions, that medications are only part of the solution, that people are still people, and psychiatrists are there to facilitate healing, compassion, acceptance, and respect. Most important is dealing with individuals on their own terms and understanding that mental illness is only one part of a person's experience. Some of these changes in the system especially affected anyone who is different and heightened the racial disparities that plague medical care. Eventually, these realizations led me toward Recovery-oriented systems of care that promote self-empowerment and are supported by human connection.

When I finished my residency (including the honor of becoming chief resident), I was offered a position as head of emergency room psychiatry. I knew this was one of the jobs reserved for the few women in the department, but I was nevertheless happy about becoming a staff member at Beth Israel Hospital, which also included an appointment at Harvard Medical School. This, my first staff position, felt familiar after my work in the state hospital but included supervising residents. I also ran an aftercare clinic for people with schizophrenia and other serious mental disorders during those early years—again deemed a second-class job, but one that was meaningful to me—and highlighted both the limitations of treatment and of resources. I also became involved in rigorous academic work, including research and writing articles for peer-reviewed medical journals.

This was when I met my future husband, another psychiatric resident, and we got married. I was fully aware of how difficult it would be to balance work and motherhood, especially from the perch of academia, but the world seemed full of possibilities. My career was flourishing, I was happily married, and my mother was doing surprisingly well. Life was busy and good.

4

The Best Laid Plans

The day I turned thirty-five, it was as if a bell rang in my head, struck by my biological clock. That morning, I went to work at Beth Israel Hospital, and without discussing my decision with anyone, I made an appointment with my department chair and gave notice that I was going to quit my job at the beginning of the summer. I was single-minded about my wish to have two children and couldn't figure out how it was possible when I was working twelve-hour days, writing on the weekends, and getting older. I was a doctor, after all, and I knew the odds; I had limited time to get pregnant without increasing the likelihood of having a baby with challenges.

Life events do not follow prescribed timelines and intentions. Fourteen years after her cancer diagnosis, I was on the telephone with my mother when she dropped the receiver and passed away. She died suddenly from disseminated intravascular coagulopathy (DIC—abnormal blood clotting), likely a long-term and rare result of the many years of chemotherapy she endured. It was the first time I saw my father cry. We were all shocked. Despite the severity of her illness, Mom had lived well, doing what she needed to do to manage. As far as I knew, she rarely allowed herself to become preoccupied or consumed by the severity of her multiple cancers or how she felt. She had many medical crises along the way, and despite the first doctor's edict, came close to fulfilling her dream: she attended the weddings of three of her four daughters and was excited about my kid sister's wedding, which she missed by only three days.

Consistent with Jewish ritual, my mother was buried two days after her death. Surprisingly, my father insisted on an open casket and gave me the choice of how she would be dressed. I chose linen shrouds, which angered her brother Bill. She didn't look real in the casket, but at least was not wearing makeup and was dressed as if she were going to Manhattan for a Broadway show.

We sat shiva at our family home in Queens. For a week, the rabbi arrived at sundown and, with a quorum of men, recited various prayers. I quietly resented how women were not included in that group, yet the activity around shiva and the comings and goings of relatives and friends helped to mitigate the shock of her death as we made it through that first week of life without my mother.

After the funeral, my husband and I went to our second home on Cape Cod and stayed there for several months. I felt strangely calm and disconnected, relieved that Mom's illness was finally over—after fourteen years of anticipating her death, it almost didn't seem real. I don't think I fully began to mourn until months later. My sense of loss surged in waves, but I had also done considerable grieving while she was alive and repeatedly hospitalized, since her death had always seemed imminent.

My biological clock continued to tick loudly, and I knew with even more certainty that I wanted to reorient my life and start a family. After leaving Beth Israel, I had been accepted to complete a fellowship at Harvard's Bunting Institute (now Radcliffe's Institute for Advanced Studies). It was a welcome respite from the constant demands of academic medicine. I fully enjoyed my two years in a non-medical setting with women from all over the country.

One Friday night I went with a close friend to downtown Boston to watch the Celtics play basketball. I felt strange but couldn't really localize it. The next morning, I developed increasingly severe abdominal pain and thought I probably had a GI virus and just needed to wait it out. But over the course of the day, I became doubled over with pain. My husband insisted we go to the ER where they did an extensive evaluation and sent me home, confirming it was a bug and I would get better. I was relieved.

At midnight, the phone rang, and the ER doctor said that I was pregnant and likely miscarrying. I needed to get to the hospital at once. I had no idea I was pregnant. I wasn't prepared for what was to come. When I got to the hospital, I was sicker because of the blood loss. We discussed with my physician whether the fetus might be viable. I had a moment of guarded excitement about the possibility. But when I saw the ultrasound, my heart broke. It became clear that I was having an ectopic pregnancy, and my abdomen had filled with blood—meaning there was no chance the fetus could survive. With little time to process what was happening and feeling both sick and sorrowful, I was rushed into emergency surgery.

I was hospitalized for about eight days, lost half my blood supply, and had a hip-to-hip incision to remove the fallopian tube where the pregnancy had settled. At first, I was too sick to process everything that had happened so suddenly—finding out I was pregnant, losing the baby, having major surgery—and then wondering what this meant for my dream of having two children. I had little energy to mourn the loss of my baby and integrate what had happened, but was glad to be alive.

From my hospital bed, my husband and I contacted an adoption agency and completed a cute scrapbook that would interest a young birth mother in us. I assumed adopting a newborn would take a few years, so we submitted the application before I was discharged. To our surprise, a birth mother in California who was due to deliver in three months chose us to be her baby's parents.

Our adoption agency conducted open adoptions, which meant the records weren't secret or sealed, so we knew our birth mother had excellent prenatal care and a good family history. The father was unknown. I thought three months would give me time to recover, but the suddenness of the adoption also helped me deny the grief I only transiently felt about the recent loss of my biological baby and the subsequent surgery, not to mention my mother's recent death.

The weeks after leaving the hospital were a blur. I was anemic and tired, but I had work responsibilities, and I became focused on setting up our baby's room, buying clothes and other necessities, and avoiding my confusing feelings. For me, action was a way of lessening the pain. Grief was mixed with excitement about becoming a parent and apprehension about how my life had changed. I focused on how, at the age of thirty-eight, I would finally have a beautiful, healthy newborn baby—a wish come true. I have been conflicted about many things in life, but never about the adoption. In my musings about Daniel, even before I saw him, I began our bonding process, imagining what it would be like to be the mom of an adorable little boy. I indulged myself in all the hopes and dreams of his bright future and my new role as a loving mother.

My husband and I got a call the day our son was born. We boarded the first available flight to Los Angeles and then drove to Orange County to meet our baby in the hospital. Daniel had a swatch of blonde hair and was swaddled in a blanket, cuddled by his birth mother. The four of us spent the day together. It felt surreal. Daniel's birth mother was young, tall, attractive, and gracious. She was only a kid yet seemed poised and certain about her decision. I imagine that giving up the baby was a wrenching choice that left a deep scar of sorrow, but it was not evident during our conversations. This was not only a searing loss for her, but the first of many traumas Daniel suffered.

I don't remember the details of that first day. I was fully focused on Daniel, snuggling him and admiring how beautiful he was. Most of all, I was adjusting to a new reality—my joy and my strong connection to this baby. As evening approached, the birth mother handed Daniel to me, and in that moment, I was fully and officially his mother. What a strange and wonderful way to become a parent! Brimming with delight, but at times riding waves of grief, my hopes were being realized.

5

Where Did My Sister Go?

Life with a newborn was everything I'd dreamed. Daniel was a delightful, active baby. The intense connection I felt with him before we met increased exponentially once we were together. I had always wanted to be a mother, and I was hooked; yet during his first year, Daniel began to manifest unusual behaviors that worried me. Most new parents have worries, so it was hard to sort out whether mine were the usual concerns of an anxious mother. However, some things were difficult to ignore. Sometimes Daniel was cuddly, and at other times unresponsive and distant, making little eye contact—he seemed strangely remote and disconnected, especially for a baby.

> *When I was very young, I have some childhood memories. I remember riding in the baby seat in the back of the car and noticing the streetlights. I also remember drinking milk from a baby bottle. I did not like switching to a glass or cup. I remember my father throwing me up into the air and catching me. I also remember the dogs my mom had—a dog named Rusty, and a dog named Obie.*

When Daniel was six months old, I took him to see my therapist Dr. John Mack, who was a tenured professor at Harvard Medical School, an experienced child psychoanalyst, a Pulitzer Prize-winning author, and, a maverick who explored alternative therapies, UFOs, and alien abduction. (Mack, 2010). Most important, Dr. Mack was compassionate, warm, supportive, and clinically astute. He gently pointed out that although Daniel was responsive at times, he "didn't feel the need to stay connected." Dr. Mack suggested we watch his development carefully. His comments left me with a pit in my stomach. I called a close friend who was a child psychologist, who reassured me but added some cautionary comments.

I didn't know what it all meant, if anything, but it felt ominous. How could my beautiful baby have serious problems?

As Daniel grew, some of his developmental landmarks were unusual, increasing my concern. He walked and used single words prior to twelve months of age, which was on the early side. At fifteen months, he climbed out of his crib and spent the night disassembling several lamps in our house. We installed locking French doors in his bedroom to keep him safe. Complicating this precocious picture, Daniel didn't need to sleep much and rarely took daytime naps. He also developed eye tics when he was about two years old. Yet, at other times he seemed like a "normal" sociable and affectionate child. It was confusing.

I was an eager mother and tried to create a loving, secure environment as well as providing opportunities that would help my son thrive. He had trouble following directions, unpredictable outbursts, and some strange behaviors. He was entranced by the water flushing in the toilet, flapping his hands with glee. His unusual behaviors were episodic and unpredictable, making any interpretation difficult. I worried about his curious development but assumed it would even out as he got older.

When Daniel was two and a half years old, we enrolled him in a Montessori preschool that met five mornings a week. He was in a class with fourteen other children. Kitty, his teacher, was supportive and very fond of Daniel. The other children liked him, and he even made friends, mitigating my worries.

He was doing well until we decided to adopt a second baby—a sibling for Daniel. After several failed attempts, our attorney found a birth mother in California. Another set of potential adoptive parents had withdrawn their papers at the last minute, so we knew there was some risk, but we had endured previous disappointments and were eager to move ahead. Daniel, my husband, and I packed up and headed to Palo Alto, where we were required to establish residence for a month to complete the first phase of the adoption. Rachel was born soon after we arrived, and we spent many happy hours with her. She was a responsive, red-headed, adorable baby. Daniel was especially connected with his little sister, loved her unconditionally, and played with her nonstop. We were such a happy family.

Once again life pitched a curveball. When it came time to leave California, we celebrated with our adoption attorney and made reservations to go home. As we packed our bags to return to Boston, we received a phone call. It was a state official at the eleventh hour, just before midnight, when this phase of the adoption would have been finalized, telling us the birth mother reclaimed the baby and placed her in foster care. There was nothing we could do. I felt powerless and stunned as a court officer arrived and took Rachel away. It was the last time we saw her.

It was late at night, and everyone was shocked and grieving. How could we have lost two babies? There was no way to explain Rachel's disappearance to Daniel. After all, she had been our child, his sister; we'd loved her, and now she was gone. The interminable flight home was a horror. It felt like someone had died, but there was no tangible way to acknowledge it or process our feelings. Daniel couldn't sit still, and it was inordinately difficult to engage him in any focused activity. I paced the aisles of the airplane with him until we finally landed, exhausted and very sad. None of us could absorb what happened, and my toddler least of all.

> *When I was a kid, we adopted Rachel. Her birth mother asked for her return. She was my sibling for a short time. Her birth mother demanded her back and sadly placed her in foster care. Her mother probably had psychological problems. We never found out what her life became.*
>
> *After the reclaiming happened, I was heartbroken. It was pure sadness I felt for months. Rachel was an almost-sibling. I felt indemnification was needed. As a kid I wanted the Wicked Witch from the Wizard of Oz to wipe out the birth mother of Rachel. I was heartbroken when she was taken away from us. I wanted Rachel back, but she was gone. I often think about her and wonder what happened to her.*

Like Daniel, decades later I still think of Rachel and what became of her. When we finally got home, we dismantled the baby's room and mobilized legal help to see if there was any possibility of reclaiming her. When word of our experience spread through the adoption network, we were offered another newborn who had been premature and a ward of the state. Her health risks paled in comparison to my dream of having a daughter, so I readily agreed. I was operating on automatic pilot and had little energy to process my confused feelings of excitement and loss. In effect, I was in a functional freeze—doing what was necessary, getting through the days.

Daniel pined for Rachel over the next several months even after we were able to adopt his new sister—on the condition set by the agency that we house a pregnant nineteen-year-old woman (not our new baby's mother) from Virginia Beach. I was required to act as her advocate until *her* baby was born and adopted by *another* family. She lived with us for about three months. Rachel was gone; Daniel experienced the joys and growing pains of *another* new baby sister; and a pregnant birth mother was moved into our house. It was chaotic for the adults, so just imagine what my son endured.

That summer with another infant—Daniel's new sibling—in the house, we sent Daniel to a morning camp program. Looking back, it was probably a mistake. He was unable to follow directions, was impulsive, agitated, and couldn't relate to the other children or staff. After three weeks, without much discussion with Daniel's father or me, he was expelled. There was no way to explain to him what happened, but he became increasingly sad and dejected.

Daniel's distress was further evident in his behavior at Montessori school that autumn. During his second year in the program, things further deteriorated. He had a challenging time following the classroom rules, was frequently distracted, restless, and unable to pay attention unless he was extremely interested in a subject. His behavior was often disruptive, particularly during transitions. He shifted between activities often, interrupted others, and engaged in physically dangerous behaviors like throwing chairs against the wall. He became more impulsive and at times verbally and physically aggressive. At other times, he would regress and become childish and giggly. According to his teachers, he was argumentative with adults, easily annoyed, spiteful, and noncompliant with requests. Further complicating this picture, Daniel had little comprehension of cause and effect. He was unable to understand how his actions impacted other people or why he was being "punished." The traumatic stresses he suffered as a baby and young child were never considered or worked through because, at the time the impact of trauma was not yet well integrated into clinical awareness.

With the help of a psychological consultant, the Montessori school designed a behavioral program, but Daniel couldn't stay with it. They suggested we follow through on their program at home, but it had little effect on his school day. Unfortunately, he gradually became seen as a "naughty boy." He seemed aware of his "bad" behavior and began feeling worse about himself, which began a cycle of remorse, hopelessness, and diminished self-esteem. By winter, he was expelled from Montessori for being unable to follow the rules.

Daniel's second expulsion before he was five years old represented another turning point. Feeling bewildered, sad, and unsure what to do next, we decided to seek professional help, which began with a neuropsychological evaluation. We didn't know it at the time, but we were entering a maze of endless psychological and educational evaluations and diagnoses we'd be trapped in for years.

Daniel was initially evaluated at Children's Hospital in Boston, then at the ADHD clinic at the University of Massachusetts Medical Center, and simultaneously by an independent behavioral therapist. My hope was that we would learn more about the causes and drivers of Daniel's difficulties and how to help him.

The University of Massachusetts evaluation was comprehensive and included input from my husband, me, and his teachers, as well as multiple sessions with Daniel. In addition to the behavioral concerns voiced by Montessori, the teachers emphasized his "inattention, impulsivity, hyperactivity, oppositional-defiant tendencies, and mild depressive symptoms." Also noted were "concerns about constant eye-blinking, as well as mouth contortions, other facial contortions, and scratching/biting himself."[1]

The evaluator concluded that Daniel's symptoms were consistent with mild to moderate Attention Deficit-Hyperactivity Disorder. ADHD is a common neurodevelopmental disorder in the United States, occurring in about four percent (3–11 percent) of children of all ages, and beginning in early childhood (Singh et al., 2015). It is frequently associated with other behavioral

---

[1]Directly from Daniel's evaluation, 1989.

disorders, especially oppositional defiant disorder and conduct disorders. Not unlike many other youngsters, Daniel's ADHD seemed to be accompanied by argumentativeness, noncompliance, and other types of oppositional tendencies. The evaluator emphasized that ADHD is a biological disorder rather than the result of environmental factors. Children with this disorder have difficulty focusing, organizing, and managing emotions. The evaluator acknowledged the psychosocial strains to which Daniel has been subjected, but he was certain that they were not the cause of his ADHD symptoms, although they may have exacerbated them.

Despite this picture, the evaluator concluded that the "prognosis for making a satisfactory adjustment to his behavioral disturbance is good because of his above-average intelligence, good relationships with peers, and the commitment of both his parents and the school staff to supporting Daniel."[2] So they labeled Daniel with ADHD and provided fairly routine recommendations for handling my four-year-old son's behavior. We went to monthly sessions to learn techniques that helped us manage Daniel's chaotic and aggressive behaviors. We were instructed to set up a time-out chair where he would sit for a prescribed period when he was out of control. When we asked him why he was in the chair, he would generally reply that he didn't know. At first, I thought he was lying, but after some years, I realized he often made no connection between cause and effect. He would kick his younger sibling, and I would tell him he needed to go to his time-out chair and calm down. It seemed he had no clue why. His problem understanding causality was undoubtedly neurological. In other words, he wasn't wired to understand the relationship between his behavior and the reason he was being put in his time-out chair. In fact, he was confused about what had happened.

We had another concern during all of this. What did it mean for Daniel now that he was slapped with a label of ADHD? Given the complexity of his challenges that slowly unfolded as he grew into adolescence, the diagnosis only further confused the picture. It's a common experience for any child who is labeled at such an early age to have ongoing difficulties in school. These

---

[2]Directly from Daniel's evaluation, 1989.

labels distort the lens through which teachers see children and through which the children see themselves, and a cycle of self-fulfilling prophecy is launched.

This was certainly the case for most of Daniel's caretakers. They focused primarily on the symptoms of ADHD. They mostly ignored his other struggles, including his escalating tics, which included making strange noises, eye blinking, and arm jerking, as well as many more phonic and motor tics over time, which adversely affected his ability to adjust to school and make friends. Similarly, they ignored his rigidity and preoccupations that were associated with various obsessions and compulsions.

Most importantly, they ignored the multiple traumas Daniel had endured during the first five years of his life. The primacy of traumatic stress and its profound impact were not fully recognized by clinicians until decades later. This was 1990; Judith Herman's seminal work, *Trauma and Recovery*, was not published until 1992; and the landmark studies by Dr. Vincent J. Felitti at Kaiser Permanente health maintenance organization and Anda at the CDC describing Adverse Childhood Experiences (ACEs) were not published until 1998 (Felitti et al., 1998). It took several more years before providers began to understand the extensiveness of traumatic experiences and their far-reaching impact and began developing an array of effective focused treatments.

As expressed by Jack Shonkoff at Harvard University's Center for the Developing Child:

> "Early experiences affect the development of brain architecture, which provides the foundation for all future learning, behavior, and health. Just as a weak foundation compromises the quality and strength of a house, *adverse experiences early in life can impair brain architecture* with negative effects lasting into adulthood" (National Scientific Council on the Developing Child, 2007). Many of these children manifest physical, emotional, and academic difficulties.

ACEs are common in the general population, and they take a toll. They include various traumatic events such as verbal, physical, and sexual abuse, domestic violence, substance abuse or mental illness of a parent, incarceration of a household member, parental separation or divorce leading to household disruption, and sudden unexpected loss. Overall, more than half of all children experience one ACE, twenty-five percent experience two or more, and one in eight experience four or more ACEs. Children with more ACEs—generally four or more—are more likely to be anxious and depressed, have various behavioral health issues such as ADHD, and experience developmental delays. As they grow into adulthood, they have a greater likelihood of developing twice the rates of cancer, heart disease, and stroke, four times the rate of chronic obstructive pulmonary disease, and are five to seven times more likely to develop substance use disorders and make suicide attempts (Burke et al., 2011; Gilbert et al., 2015; Harris, 2023; Unick et al., 2019).

By the time Daniel was three years old, he had endured many events that contributed to his ACE score: the primal loss of his birth mother, the adoption, Rachel's disappearance, the mysterious appearance and then disappearance of the pregnant birth mother we housed, teachers who punished and humiliated him, and his expulsions from summer camp and Montessori. Not only was childhood trauma not being addressed back then, but the impact of historical traumas—the dynamics and culture of loss Daniel inherited from our families, as well as his biological parents—were likely contributing factors. He was a victim of a diagnostic system that is biomedically based and doesn't adequately account for the impact of environment, culture, and psychosocial stressors.

Before he had even entered kindergarten, our family and especially Daniel were stuck in the epicenter of serious and unpredictable events, and there was no way to adequately process them. How much of my son's behavior, sadness, and dejection resulted from these profound losses and were expressions of his grief? What might have happened if Daniel's traumatic history had been acknowledged and addressed? I wonder whether his course would have been different if we had known more about post-traumatic stress disorder (PTSD) and its treatment and focused on the impact of his losses and his grief rather than on ADHD and his behavioral symptoms—symptoms that very well may have been expressions of his grief. Instead, the findings from the first evaluation from the University of Massachusetts foreshadowed what was to come. Furthermore, his tic disorder—which would later fully manifest as

Tourette Syndrome—and his obsessive-compulsive symptoms—OCD—were ignored.

It was a lot, but we were only beginning our journey of labels, often-conflicting multiple diagnoses, confusion, and sorrow. Daniel's experience from the time he was three years old through the sixth grade would become a nightmare of escalating humiliation, defeat, and ultimately despair.

6

How the System Failed Daniel

Once my son came to be seen as a "bad boy with bad behavior," it was a label he was unable to shake. He was moved around from classroom to classroom, school to school, and his placements became increasingly restrictive. Looking back at Daniel's records, I can see he was set up for failure from the beginning. Even though as a psychiatrist I had never encountered anyone quite like him, I wasn't alarmed at first because kids are quirky, yet as time went on, I dreaded the possibility of institutionalization, which was regularly threatened by the school system.

It is important to remember that I never knew (and never will know) first-hand what happened during Daniel's early education and only witnessed the considerable stresses Daniel faced and expressed at home. I wasn't there for the school day except when I was called to pick him up because he was deemed unmanageable. As a result, I have relied primarily on second-hand information I've gathered and considered: school records containing teacher's notes, Individualized Education Programs (IEPs), minutes from school and parent meetings, consultants' observations and recommendations, and what Daniel remembered about his experiences. Most of my information came from the required and difficult IEP meetings that included school staff, teachers, and parents. I was asked to sign off on the IEPs despite their shortcomings. It seemed futile not to, even though the schools' capacity to implement the stated goals seemed questionable. The staff frequently questioned my parenting ability, fully shifting the responsibility for Daniel's difficult behavior to me.

Daniel attended four different local schools during those early years—Heath, Driscoll, Runkle, and Manville—starting with a mainstream kindergarten class with a full-time aide, moving on to more restrictive settings, and ultimately ending up in sixth grade in a school solely for children who had disabilities. With rare exceptions, teachers and staff were so focused on keeping him in his seat and managing his odd behavior and progressively worsening tics that the underlying issues were obscured. As a result, they no longer prioritized teaching, helping him learn, or making friends, which is the whole point of early education in the first place. Instead, he was increasingly isolated and punished.

Before he even set foot in kindergarten, he was singled out and deemed a problem the school staff had trouble solving—not as a bright but quirky kid with underlying trauma and neurological issues. His preschool behavioral consultant recommended a standard core evaluation before kindergarten to help the district determine if Daniel required special education services. His father and I complied. As a result, because various school options were unavailable, Daniel was shunted around to different programs that spring, all of them concluding there was no room for him, or they couldn't manage a student like him. He missed more than half a year of elementary school due to the process of determining where he should go to school.

Toward the completion of the core evaluation period, Daniel was observed for two weeks in a kindergarten class at a neighborhood public school. Although we were repeatedly reassured this was a "no-failure diagnostic," this introduction to the school he ultimately attended paved the way for a faulty and inauspicious beginning. The kindergarten classroom teacher had trouble integrating a strange new student, and the school observer had little familiarity with children who may have ADHD. Daniel was introduced to the other students as a "visitor." Due to no fault of his own, Daniel was extruded from the group, misattributions were made about his behavior, and from the very beginning, he was viewed through a lens of deficit. The teacher described Daniel as "socially and emotionally unaware . . . I see a flat affect . . . there's simply a kind of resignation but no excitement, happiness, or sadness that is evident." It is not surprising that Daniel shut down to manage all the transitions, instability, and multiple evaluations. And he wasn't even six years old.

Throughout these elementary years, as treatments were adjusted, plans rewritten, and schools changed, Daniel began his travels down a disastrous course that grew progressively more difficult and ultimately impossible to return from. His disruptive behaviors, often the result of his uncontrollable tics, overshadowed his strengths, superior intelligence, sweetness, and considerable capabilities. An early consultant described him as:

> A bright, highly verbal, boy with a well-developed fund of knowledge, particularly in the sciences. He is inquisitive, responds to reinforcement, and is quite agile. His inquisitiveness is a challenge to any teacher willing to go beyond traditional curricula designs. He responds to consistent limits and works well in a one-to-one small group setting.

Even in the first and second grades, he was further described as having a

> unique understanding of the world around him and an engaging sense of humor. His insights when appropriately presented command positive attention and respect from peers. Daniel brings a wealth of knowledge and experience. His expertise is helpful as a springboard for instruction and as a vehicle for social recognition.

None of these qualities seemed to matter much to teachers who had limited resources and were trying to control a classroom, and so positive views of Daniel became increasingly infrequent as the school years went by. They were overshadowed by extensive reports of his impulsivity, distractibility, hyperactivity, poor frustration tolerance, verbal and motor disinhibition, and "baby talk," sometimes ending in inappropriate actions such as non-compliance, ignoring rules, and occasionally becoming physically aggressive and even throwing furniture. These descriptions from the school, especially in the early reports, tended to focus on symptoms rather than addressing the causes or how best to integrate him into the classroom. I began to dread picking him up at the end of the day because of the disparaging things I was told about him. It's no wonder he was so sad and defeated.

Within this elementary school period, Daniel's tic disorder escalated. He had motor and phonic tics; he went from eye blinking to shoulder shrugging, grimacing, and torso jerking. At times, these were accompanied by vocalizations, such as raucous giggling, grunting, silly verbalizations, spitting, screaming, or making strange noises, and as he grew older, by swearing or repeating other peoples' words (echolalia). All the evaluators over the years seemed to agree that when he was stressed, the tics became worse, and although variable, were indeed disturbing. He had no control over them.

By the time Daniel was seven years old, not only was he adapting to a new baby sibling, but our entire family was also reeling from my husband's and my divorce after nineteen years of marriage—another major trauma for all of us that was inadequately processed. That's also when Daniel was diagnosed with Tourette Syndrome (TS), a neurodevelopmental disorder, along with obsessive compulsive disorder (OCD) which emerged at about the same time. The tics and Tourette symptoms overrode some of his other behavioral issues because they were so dramatic and disruptive, and schools had no adequate way of dealing with them. This continued until adolescence because, as Daniel puts it, he had no choice but to "listen to his brain."

This was the beginning of Daniel having an ever-evolving treatment team that continues to this day. We hired a behavioral consultant who was extremely present for years even after Daniel was finished with traditional schooling—Dr. James Keefe. He was a schoolteacher with a strong knowledge of behavioral strategies, and Daniel really liked him and would phone him when he was upset. Daniel also saw a psychiatrist who was "treating" his Tourette Syndrome with medication—Dr. Barbara Coffey—and a psychotherapist named Bob Brooks, who helped him convey his experience in his story of the "Tourette Monster."

Once upon a time there was a boy named John. John was very mad because he was bothered by the Tourette Monster. The Tourette Monster got him to do crazy things like fart in people's faces, and at people. John didn't really want to do this, but the Tourette Monster made him do it. People got angry with John because of the things he did. John got sad because people didn't like him.

Some people knew that John had Tourette's, and he did crazy things and lot of weird things because he had Tourette's, but they also knew he was a really nice person. Some people really didn't understand that he had Tourette's, or they didn't understand about Tourette's so they thought that maybe they shouldn't even be friends with John.

Sometimes John got very worried about how he would be when he got older. He was worried that he would still do bad things like pull down his pants in school or get kicked out of his job. This made him feel bad. John didn't know what he could do to make things better. John's parents knew he felt unhappy, and they told him about Dr. Wiggle (Bob Brooks). Dr. Wiggle helped kids with TS. First, he did not want to see Dr. Wiggle and then later he wanted to see him even more.

One way that Dr. Wiggle helped John was to give him pills. The pills made the Tourette Monster sick so he couldn't make the kid do as much bad things. Dr. Wiggle also talked with John about his TS and gave him good ideas about stopping his Tourette behavior and behaving better. Dr. Wiggle told John that it wasn't easy but that he should try to think about what he was doing.

John tried to remember what Dr. Wiggle said. But once when he was in school the Tourette Monster told John's brain to tell John to pull down his pants. John did it but then felt bad. John wanted to figure out a way not to have his brain listen to the Tourette Monster. The pills helped but he knew that he had to do other things also because he didn't want people to be angry with him. John really wanted people to be his friends.

One day John felt so bad about having the Tourette Monster that he thought the only way he could kill the Tourette Monster was to kill himself. He told Dr. Wiggle how he felt. Dr. Wiggle said he was very sorry that John felt that way. he said to John that he can't get rid of the Tourette Monster, but he could eventually learn to have his brain learn not to listen to the Tourette Monster. John felt happy when Dr. Wiggle said that.

Despite our best efforts, Daniel spent second and third grades at the Driscoll School, where he was taken out of the mainstream and assigned a 502.4 placement; this meant that more than sixty percent of his time was in special education. He had a full-time aide and was in a separate class with four other boys with disabilities. He recalled the period as relatively benign.

> *When I was at Driscoll school there was a teacher named Ginger. She was a good teacher. I made friends with another kid who was poor and lived in the projects. I was not bullied. However not everyone was friendly to me. Me and my new friend would talk trash about another kid, but I soon found he was picked on, so I ceased the trash talking immediately because it was not fair.*

The teacher Daniel mentions is Virginia Watkins, who described him in third grade, writing:

> Danny's behavior in the classroom has run the full gamut from gentle kindness toward a preferred teacher or friend to spitting in a classmate's face; from a pleasant greeting and verbal sharing of concrete personal experiences to the screaming of racial or obscene epithets; from exaggerated seeking of personal privacy to exposing himself and or engaging in obscene gestures and body movements; from calm and attentive learning in a small group to a full-blown physical attack on the person closest to him.
>
> It has been variously suggested that Danny's behaviors are the result of (unplanned) interferences with his personal thoughts (obsessions); that many of these behaviors are simple or complex, verbal or physical tics (including the possibility of rage tics); that they are the result of anxiety, with all its physiological con-commitments; that they are associated with physical or on-task fatigue; that they are limit testing and or avoidance techniques; in that they are associated with unexpressed, but developmentally appropriate, concerns. It is probable that all these explanations are valid at varying times.

And she was clearly fond of him:

> Danny is a truly "poignant" child—a child who is keenly distressing yet appealing to the emotions; a child who can pierce one, yet be skillful; astute, intense, sharp, or pungent to the senses.
>
> Danny is a bright child, whose neurobehavioral and neuropsychological disabilities cause him, and everyone around him, both sadness and distress. While it is eminently clear that each and every member of his team, parent

> and professional alike, is working to assist Danny to override the discrepancy between his intellectual capabilities and his interfering behaviors (be they neurologically, emotionally, or environmentally induced), it is also true that none of us has yet found "the key to success." Danny feels our failures quite deeply; But is not yet willing to reformulate the issue and take responsibility for his own success, albeit, given sufficient and appropriate help.

Despite her optimism, there's a sad prescience in her summation, and it seemed to me that Daniel was already doomed—especially since the school had limited resources.

> Danny will require continued and extensive assistance from all members of his team, working in concert to build appropriate self-esteem, manage his behaviors, and develop grade-level academic and social skills (V. Watkins [school assessment], personal communication, 1992).

During his third-grade year, Daniel's out-of-control behavior escalated. One of his classmates had a chronic runny nose, and Daniel was germ-phobic—a manifestation of his OCD. The two boys liked to play chess, but Daniel would become agitated when his classmate touched his nose and then the chess pieces. Sometimes, Daniel threw the chessboard and ran out of the classroom, and occasionally out of the building. The school's method of managing this problem was to take his shoes away in the morning, which, of course further humiliated and othered him and did nothing to redirect or change his behavior.

> *When I was about eight years old, I was in the third grade. I was exhibiting behavioral problems due to my diagnosis of Tourette syndrome. My behavioral outbursts consisted of constant grimacing and uncontrollable laughter that constantly interrupted the class. Because of my behavioral outbursts I was sent to a special timeout room in which the walls were painted in a jungle theme.*
>
> *I was not the only kid often kept in this "special" timeout room. I had trouble paying attention in class when I was in class. The other kids had it out for me, picked on me, and I got into a fight, but I stood up to the other kid and he stopped. Another kid was beaten up badly and I felt terrible about this, yet I could do nothing because the kids who were picking on this kid*

> *were bigger than me. The school had a playground where I would have lots of fun, especially on the swing set. I would see how high I could go. There were frequent fire drills, and everybody would calmly walk out into the school parking lot.*

Although he was already in a restricted classroom that was not fully integrated with the rest of the school, he was frequently "managed" by being put into timeout. The school used restraints to deal with his tic behavior and his obsessions. Daniel told me the female staff generally confined him by sitting on him, while the male teachers used their legs to hold his shoulders down. Remember, he was eight or nine years old and at the time was a skinny small kid. It's no surprise Daniel felt restricted and isolated, but he coped in his own ways.

> *The times I was left alone in the timeout room I would move the ceiling panels and crawl into the ceiling to see what was in the science room. The science room had ferrets. I found this to be very interesting. After I spied on what the students were doing I would jump down from the ceiling onto the floor of the timeout room.*

In the spring of third grade, we withdrew Daniel from school for the rest of the year because, as he put it, "I wasn't learning much, and I spent too much time alone in the time-out room."

In fourth grade, Daniel was transferred to yet another school—Runkle—as his behaviors became increasingly unpredictable. Yet at times, he functioned well, especially considering the key traumatic stressors in our home environment during these years. Not only were there considerable adjustments as I became a single parent of two challenging children, but we also endured a catastrophic electrical fire that burned down one-third of our house.

On a snowy night in February, I awoke to a smoke-filled room and the fire alarms blaring. When I opened my bedroom door, I was blanketed with thick smoke, so I ran to wake up my children, grabbed them along with my dogs, and got all of us out of the house and away from the flames. Despite the snow on the ground, I wasn't wearing any shoes. The fire galloped through the house since we had polyurethane wooden floors, but I felt huge relief knowing that my children were okay and the police were kindly searching for my dogs who had jumped the fence in fear. The firefighters came in with hoses, broke most of the windows, and threw away all the bedding. They took almost all our clothes to clean and stripped the house since it was smoke-damaged. I found out much later that the fire was started by an electric can opener that sat unused on the kitchen counter but was plugged in; they believed a power surge started the fire and it had crept up the walls and through the house. Everything in the kitchen was destroyed. Not one glass, dish, pot, or fork was left. All that remained of one side of our home was a pile of rubble, but nobody was hurt, and the police found my two golden retrievers.

Because I had become increasingly adept at compartmentalizing my own fear and distress, I went to a work meeting the next evening smelling like a barbecue. I felt obligated to go since people had traveled from out of town. Meanwhile, the kids stayed with their loving grandmother for a brief period. I remained at home with my dogs while cleaners came to wash the smoke-damaged walls. One-third of the house remained boarded up for part of a year while the kitchen and adjacent rooms were rebuilt. When the kids moved back home, they enjoyed the many nights of pizza and fast food we cooked in a microwave and ice cream from a small refrigerator that I bought. I had little space to properly grieve this disaster; my overriding feeling was relief, although now, looking back at the danger and damage, I can see my denial as well.

That's what Daniel was coping with when he began fifth grade. A trained aide skilled in behavioral management and with knowledge of Tourette Syndrome saw that Daniel did well with frequent breaks and opportunities to "chat about personal interests and concerns" and implemented them. During this period, he joined the mainstream students for gym and art and enjoyed a structured curriculum around his interests in science and nature. The teacher emphasized that Daniel was "motivated to learn and do well by a desire to participate and keep up with other class members and by his keen interest in acquiring and expanding his knowledge."

Despite these glimmers of hope intermixed with relatively calm and productive times, his disturbing behavior escalated. An extreme but not atypical episode occurred when Daniel suddenly began running around the school—racing up and down the stairs. One of the aides tried to restrain him, and Daniel resisted. He swore, laughed raucously, and yelled. The aide tried to control Daniel, but he headbutted and kicked him. As my son was dragged toward a classroom, he dropped down limp, so he had to be carried to an empty office. Not surprisingly, Daniel trashed the office, pulling posters off the walls and throwing a chair. It was unclear what precipitated the episode—if anything—but it was not unusual for Daniel to occasionally run out of the classroom into the street. I became so worried that he would get hit by a car that I took him to a behavioral consultant who recommended a trip to the local cemetery at night where I pointed out gravestones where children had supposedly been hit by cars and died. It frightened Daniel; his behavior improved, but I regretted resorting to such a manipulative measure.

A version of this scenario was repeated more times than I can count. Although we hired myriad consultants to help, almost all of them told us the school was misinformed about TS. They felt Daniel's teachers and aides were using timeout and restraints excessively and treating Daniel's tic behavior as intentional and controllable by him, rather than a neurodevelopmental disorder that peaked during this period.

Daniel became increasingly traumatized by his school experiences, so in the spring of fifth grade we once again withdrew him when things got out of hand. We hoped it would be temporary because he was lonely, defeated, and dejected at home, and despite a competent tutor, we felt he would be better off in a classroom with peers.

The general view of disabilities is spelled out in the Individuals with Disabilities Education Act (IDEA), including many updates from 2004, which requires states to provide public education for students aged three to twenty-one, no matter how severe their disabilities. In this law, Congress states:

> Disability is a natural part of the human experience and in no way diminishes the right of individuals to participate in or contribute to society. Improving educational results for children with disabilities is an essential element of our national policy of ensuring equality of opportunity, full participation,

> independent living, and economic self-sufficiency for individuals with disabilities (U.S. Department of Education, 2004).

However, it is important to note that only minimal guidelines about how these principles should be implemented were available when Daniel was in school. The best way to understand how his elementary educators hoped to respond to Daniel's difficult and sometimes disruptive behaviors is to review his Individualized Education Plans. "The Individuals with Disabilities Education Act mandates that free, appropriate, public education (FAPE) be provided to children with educationally defined disabilities. The Individualized Education Program (IEP) requirement (i.e., team meeting and document) is the method for providing FAPE to children" (Simon, 2006). The IEP describes each student's current performance level, goals and objectives, and the teaching approach, methodology, and monitoring needed to fulfill these goals. Achievement of these objectives is then rated during each quarter of the school year. The IEPs, combined with the teachers' summaries of Daniel's behaviors and consultant's observations, recreate the attitudes and practices of the staff and help us better understand what happened to Daniel during elementary school.

Examples of objectives from Daniel's IEP track the course of his deterioration, which may or may not have led to his eventual psychotic break. His IEP from second grade included:

- Given a positive relationship with the teacher, Daniel will behave appropriately within the class.
- Given a conflict situation, Daniel will interact appropriately with school authority figures.
- Given a class setting, Daniel will interact appropriately with one student of the same sex three times during the class.

By fifth grade:

- Given a situation, Daniel will be encouraged to verbally process what occurred with a sensitive adult 90 percent of the time.

- Given a transition, Daniel will follow learned routines promptly and quietly 90 percent of the time.
- During all class sessions, Daniel will use an appropriate communicative volume when speaking 95 percent of the time.
- During all class sessions, Daniel will use appropriate language to obtain an adult's attention 90 percent of the time.

How were these objectives going to be implemented? As I was writing this book and, with the benefit of hindsight, reviewed the IEPs, I solicited expert input from an experienced special education teacher who reviewed the materials. Together, we concluded that the plans were strikingly deficient. However, our impressions were subjective. The IEPs, written during Daniel's early years in elementary school, seemed to be based on computer-generated, standardized, and pre-written goals, which were the trend during that period. They were not personalized, did not specifically address Daniel's unique needs and history, and were focused almost entirely on deficits without attention to strengths. Many of the objectives were laudable, but how was one to implement adequate management strategies?

The teaching approach and methodology, especially from first to fourth grades, did not spell out what and how Daniel should be taught. For example: *How does the instructor develop a positive relationship with Daniel? What does it consist of? And given Daniel's tics, what constitutes "appropriate" behavior?* Similarly, there is little attention paid to the skills needed by the aide and how this staff person should be trained. What is the definition of "sensitive adult"? The instructional strategies seemed focused on compliance-related development, frequent reinforcement, or punitive consequences rather than on specific positive approaches, strategies, and skills that Daniel and the staff needed to address his challenging behaviors, including his tic disorder.

The stated goals regarding socialization were equally vague, and the sequence in which the school planned to teach these critical skills was problematic. Throughout the IEPs, it was clearly identified that Daniel had difficulty with relationships, anxiety, and self-esteem. The plan was for Daniel to "develop a working relationship with the counselor" and identify general areas in which he was having difficulty. Once these were achieved, the plan was for him to "develop strategies to resolve the specific problems," test these strategies, and "revise as needed." He was set up to fail because the teaching strategies necessary to achieve the stated goals were not clearly articulated, nor were the resources to implement them generally available. What did they plan to teach Daniel that would help him cope, interact successfully, and enable him to be in a state of mind where he could learn? Why would they have him focusing on identifying his problems before teaching him how to deal with these situations?

Happily, in recent years, evidence-based instructional strategies have been developed. For example, techniques that support smooth transitions might include verbal cues such as "Five minutes until recess begins" or visual cues describing the next activity. Yet in Daniel's IEPs, spelling out specific strategies with clarity was largely absent. Most importantly, although there was consensus throughout the reports that Daniel needed a full-time one-on-one trained aide, resource constraints, disagreement about Daniel's needs, fuzzy guidelines for mainstreaming versus exclusion, and perhaps school politics prevented this from occurring consistently. Many of the classroom supports—the teachers' assistants—were inadequately trained and misunderstood Daniel's behaviors, especially his tic disorder, which was seen as volitional rather than neurodevelopmental.

In lieu of a trained aide, time-out was implemented. In the first grade, the time-out chair was in the main stairwell where other students regularly passed by, humiliating Daniel. One of the behavioral consultants addressed this issue in concrete terms.

> Daniel's placement should have an area where he can go and release some of his anxiety with the help of his monitor and double as a time-out place. This must be a place that is in close proximity to the classroom—this proximity being less than 50 feet from his classroom but should not be a hall or a closet. This should all be done under the auspices of a selected containment and protection policy agreed upon by parents and staff around issues such as silliness and inappropriate behaviors (e.g., grimacing, flapping arms, agitation, silly verbalizations, toileting language, aggression, and acting out). It was also generally recommended that to

ensure adequate communication between home and school, a notebook describing his daily accomplishments and difficulties should be passed back and forth.

None of this was ever carried out. A behavioral management program was the backbone of most of the consultants' and evaluators' recommendations. When Daniel was eight years old and in third grade, the evaluator concluded the following and suggested that these strategies be integrated into his IEPs:

> This child presents a challenge with respect to his educational and program needs. . . . However, given that his intelligence testing, which is the most predictive index of school achievement, falls in the superior range, I would recommend that this serve as a central guidepost in developing an appropriate IEP and in determining his placement. However, given that his needs have necessitated a 1:1 aide in the past, it would appear that his current educational placement in a small class with frequent opportunities for small group and individualized instruction is appropriate. In addition, the program offers teaching staff who can be flexible in response to his, at times, inflexible stance and be able to provide the emotional support which he will require in order to be successful.

Eventually, Dr. Keefe, our major behavioral consultant, supported this perspective and recommended a behavioral management plan that was overseen by a trained one-on-one aide and included:

- Enhance Daniel's self-esteem, cognitive flexibility, and social relatedness through positive reinforcement; avoid punishment and negative consequences.
- Facilitate his ability to label and verbalize his feelings.
- Prepare him for all activities and transitions.
- Incorporate a system for home, school, and medical specialists that ensures regular communication.
- Use computers to bypass his graphomotor weakness.

How were these IEP strategies translated and implemented in the classroom on a daily basis?

They weren't.

Furthermore, some of these strategies, such as processing his feelings (if that were really possible in a boy this young), might have mitigated some of the tic storms but would not have prevented them or their impact on Daniel and the people around him. Instead, the IEPs should have focused on how to manage his major disruptive behaviors and symptoms that at this point included inattention, impulsive behavior, motor and vocal tics, and aggressive behavior. For example, Daniel's TS doctor suggested the school set up a "tic room" or "tic space" for de-stimulation, but this was never done.

In retrospect, it is glaringly clear that the IEPs had multiple critical deficiencies. For example, rather than the school teaching the students about TS and including Daniel in how that might be approached, it was largely ignored. Although the schools received input from various TS experts, they did not integrate much of it into their classroom teaching.

Rather than acknowledging Daniel's major neurological problem often triggered by stressful situations, many of the teachers wrote things like "Daniel was extraordinarily lucky insofar as his classmates have been generous in their forgiveness and kindness toward him." The teachers did little to decrease the perceived necessity for forgiving my child for having a disability. His peers may have been kind, but it belies the school's neglect.

They perceived Daniel as a problem that needed fixing rather than a little boy who was struggling to grow up, manage his disability, cope, and be part of a community. His considerable abilities were largely ignored, and his inherent sweetness and kindness, as well as his considerable interests in science and nature, for example, were occasionally mentioned but overshadowed by his difficulties. Furthermore, the IEPs focused on goals and objectives and only occasionally spelled out the specific teaching methods or instructional strategies necessary to address them. The supports they described gave little to no attention to the world as Daniel experienced it but rather applied a formulaic approach anchored by behavioral management and punitive strategies.

The school psychologist who ran a small social skills group when Daniel was in the fifth grade stated the following, which suggested that if the management of Daniel had followed some of the IEP recommendations, he might have done better.

> It has been important for Daniel to have adults around him that are sensitive and attuned to his needs and can quickly discern the slightest upsetting sign of distress before giving it a chance to escalate into out-of-control behavior. He has responded well to expectations spelled out in advance; to a calm firm tone of voice when he needed feedback during inappropriate behavior; to professionals who engage him intellectually for problem solving about the available choices. Daniel has been able to bounce back whenever there is acknowledgment of his abilities, and an appeal was made to his friendship needs. He has benefitted from acceptance, praise and sensitivity communicated to him through immediate positive feedback. He has thrived on efforts to bolster his self-worth and self-esteem. (personal communication, 1994)

The later IEPs, like the one above, were more personalized and included some of the skills and critical teaching methods needed to help Daniel grow and thrive, but it was far too little and too late. And without specific attention to TS, the harm had been done. Daniel's self-esteem and confidence were eroded, and with them, his behavior, which deteriorated over his years in elementary school to such a degree that it led to his most disastrous experience yet: Manville.

7

"I Didn't Go to School; I Only Went to Timeout"

By sixth grade, Daniel was enrolled in his fifth school—Manville, a therapeutic private school for children with disabilities. Manville was part of Boston's respected Judge Baker Children's Center, affiliated with Harvard University, and dedicated to improving the quality of children's mental health care "by translating research into programs and services that change lives" (The Baker Center for Children and Families, 2021). We readily agreed to Daniel's transfer, mistakenly believing Manville would understand Daniel's behaviors, provide necessary one-on-one support when necessary, and at the same time appreciate his capabilities and deal with him compassionately and skillfully.

We were dead wrong.

Rather than understanding Daniel's difficult behaviors as part of a serious neurological illness that he couldn't control, he was seen as a bad kid who needed to be punished to become more compliant. These views were a microcosm of the general societal views of people who are vulnerable and different; in clinical terms he was neurodivergent, not a bad kid. A teacher described this time in his life, writing:

> Dan entered the Manville School in September 1995. He presented as an extremely anxious boy unsure of what to expect from his new school environment. He exhibited disorganized and somewhat disinhibited behaviors. After the first few months he appeared to begin to trust adults

and would reach out in small increments to both adults and peers. He began to participate in academic and social activities more frequently. He received praise in a November meeting with his mother, therapist, counselor, teacher, and the director for his improvement.

After the December vacation, his behaviors appeared more sexualized. Dan's counselor and therapist discussed their concerns with him and explored the reasons for this behavior. Dan continued to become more disorganized in class, and his sexualized talk and aggressive behaviors increased (see therapist report). He was able to remain in class only one out of five school days, actively engage in class for 1/2 to 1 1/2 hours out of five days, and appeared sedated one out of seven days. He needed one-on-one instruction with a variety of options and interventions that would enable him to participate in reading, writing, and hands-on academic tasks.

As Daniel remembers it, he was put in four-point restraints at least twice a day. The most common triggers were strange episodes he had where he would begin to raucously giggle and couldn't stop—often disrupting classroom activities. This tic related to TS was often coupled with bizarre grimaces and body movements. Somehow, the school staff had little understanding of TS and, like his elementary schools, viewed it not as a significant neurological disorder but as one that was in Daniel's control and the result of "emotional problems."

In addition to the very frequent restraints, Daniel was often isolated in a small classroom where he sat all day long, generally doing nothing. He described the aides flicking their fingers on his head and feeling helpless and worthless. Daniel said that he was rarely with the other kids.

When I was eleven years old, I was sent to a school called Manville. At Manville they man-handled me. They would act in terrifying ways and take inappropriate actions toward me. They would cut snippets of my hair, flick their fingers on my head to annoy me, and slam my head onto the desk. They would also bring my arms forcibly around my back which hurt. I often spent the day with my head on the desk doing nothing. They put me in rooms with 'nasty kids' for fun just to see what would happen. I was terrified and incredibly angry. I kept thinking that if I had a gun, I would shoot one of the abusive staff.

Daniel was despairing, as was I. The school outright blamed me for his behavior during our meetings and insisted I was too fused with him and spent too much time with him—how could it have been otherwise? My child felt worthless, excluded, abused, lacked confidence, was lonely, and isolated. Then, according to a teacher,

> During Dan's last month in school, he was unable to stay in class for more than fifteen minutes at a time before he became very disinhibited both verbally and physically. On his last day he appeared to be calm, and, while engaged in examining a flip book (in preparation for an upcoming activity), without any provocation stabbed the boy sitting next to him with a pencil, breaking the skin. After this incident Dan was suspended for two days and, due to parent decision, never returned to school.

What is left out of this report are two major events. First, the truth about the "stabbing" incident. Second, that the school recommended institutionalizing my son. These events are vividly imprinted in my mind. I was sitting at my desk at work, absorbed in a manuscript, when Jayne Samuda, my very capable assistant and good friend, burst into my office and blurted out that she had just gotten a call from Daniel's school. "They're saying he stabbed someone!" I froze, unable to speak, overwhelmed by images of police, blood, and Daniel being carted off to Bridgewater State Hospital, one of my most persistent fears.

It turned out the "stabbing" had occurred when Daniel had poked a fellow student in the arm with a pencil without apparent provocation. He was examining a book and had seemed calm. The other student had a small puncture wound on his upper arm requiring a band-aid. The school staff was agitated, demanding an immediate meeting. When I heard that he had not knifed someone and hurt them, I cried with relief and anger. I asked Jayne to call my ex-husband to let him know about the meeting.

The next afternoon we all met at Manville. We gathered around a large conference table in a lifeless classroom with bare pale green walls and dim light. Various teachers and administrators sat rigidly in their uncomfortable chairs, avoiding eye contact as they questioned Daniel's father and my ability to manage him. The administration had many complaints: Daniel was not engaged in their program, his behaviors were disruptive, he had no relationship with other students or with the teachers, and he didn't listen. He was generally quiet, but also unpredictable, restless, easily agitated, and distractible, and they didn't know how to get him to conform to the formal structure of their school day. Again, remember, this was a therapeutic private school for children with disabilities, not the neighborhood public school.

As in prior IEP meetings, the school had spelled out their many frustrations with Daniel and all the ways he was different and didn't fit in. There was little left to say. I knew his differences and aberrant behaviors all too well but also knew that he could be engaged and involved in trusting relationships. I remained silent, awaiting the inevitable ultimatum, although I wasn't sure what it would be this time.

The Manville School administration proclaimed that Daniel needed to be reevaluated and placed in a residential facility.

Repressing my rage and disappointment, I simply stated, "No, that is not the solution."

As a mother, I refused to seriously entertain this option. As a psychiatrist, I was aware of the considerable drawbacks of residential mental health placement and would not subject my son to them. I also knew that because of the Brookline school district's legal obligation to provide services, it was within my rights to request that a home-schooling program be created and provided for Daniel. My ex-husband agreed with this strategy.

When I got home and told Daniel he no longer had to go back to school, he breathed a big sigh of relief, smiled, and said, "It doesn't matter, Mom. I didn't go to school anyway; I only went to time out."

Despite his unpredictable behavior, Daniel's warm sweetness, intelligence, and lack of guile combined with his strikingly good looks were at times more than I could bear. Once again, I was heartbroken. How could I better protect and support Daniel? Was he so different that it was impossible to educate him? What would happen to my son?

Part II

Descent into Psychosis

8

Isolated and Lonely

According to Daniel's IEP and team negotiations with the Brookline school system, his placement when he was eleven years old was for schooling in our home for one year, but Daniel never went to regular school again, although he intermittently attended various therapeutic day school programs. He often seemed lonely and was excluded from other children and usual routines, but homeschooling meant he was no longer demeaned, bullied, or worse. He says he felt protected and had some autonomy.

Putting together a comprehensive school program and curriculum with a compassionate, knowledgeable staff at home, especially as a single mother raising two children and working full time (at this point as president of a non-profit for homeless families and their children), was challenging. It was even more difficult to find ways for Daniel to socialize with peers. The Department of Education sent a steady stream of expert consultants who were unable to implement a comprehensive educational program that integrated academics with socialization.

When I was homeschooled, I was very bored with everything, but I was finally free after Manville. I took it easy. I would just walk from one room in my house to another and sometimes wander around the neighborhood. My homeschool tutors taught me what a normal school curriculum was like. I learned some, just enough to keep up with what other kids would have been learning. I would often go to Starbucks. I started taking the T around as well. I had a case manager to call if anything was upsetting me. I liked going with the tutors to get pizza or Mexican food. Occasionally I would climb Blue Hills Mountain where I would hike. I spent long times in my room playing computer games to kill time. I had few friends and was lonely. I remember sleeping in a lot and had trouble getting up in the morning as my biological clock got thrown off. I would then read some books and do the occasional math or literature for my homeschool tasks. Another activity was to ride my bicycle around the neighborhood. No one manhandled me like they did at Manville. I was free.

My homeschool tutors were Brad, Aaron, and Albert. They were very nice people. They would teach me all the subjects. Brad would take me to the park and have me write in a journal. With Aaron I would hang out at the local pizza joint. Albert focused on math. Aaron and Albert became family friends. We stayed in contact for years to come.

Although it was difficult to enforce a routine, we intuitively employed people who were compassionate and didn't see Daniel as a diagnostic label. The most important were Aaron, a schoolteacher, and Albert, a student at Boston College, who had grown up in South Central LA. Neither were affiliated with the mental health system and instead saw Daniel as a lonely kid struggling to grow up. They tried to support him in seeing himself as a valued kid and, as Daniel described, not a "psycho or freak." He was just a preadolescent boy with challenges.

This team helped Daniel do his best to meet the objectives for his program, which was spelled out in the annual IEPs. Like the IEPs in elementary school, they specified various goals as well as evaluation procedures and a timetable for implementation. They were primarily focused on Daniel's academic skills rather than his behavioral and social issues. These tended to be more personalized than in elementary school but still did not address how the objectives could be successfully carried out. The following IEP from Daniel's second year at home, when he was thirteen years old, is a good example of the shortcomings of these plans.

Goal 1.3: Through modifications, strategies and external support, Daniel will improve his social pragmatic skills.

Objective 1.3.1: Daniel with support, will learn specific problem solving and social conflict resolution strategies to increase appropriate interaction with adults and peers.

Objective 1.3.2: Daniel with support will increase his time in community social activities. He will learn appropriate community norms and strategies to deal with feeling overwhelmed.

Objective 1.3.3: Daniel with staff support will increase his time in small group academics by using pragmatic skills and social cues.

Objective 1.3.4: Daniel with support will improve his self-esteem and self-image.

Evaluation Procedure: Teacher observation, Expectation sheet data, analysis of videotapes

Evaluation Schedule: Weekly, monthly, quarterly reports.

These are all laudable aspirations, but they do not spell out the skills and time the staff needs to accomplish them. What constitutes support? How would Daniel learn these skills? What training did the staff need to teach Daniel conflict resolution, community norms, or the rest of the list? How does this translate into improved self-esteem, especially given his prior traumatic experiences in school? The specific skills and the steps necessary were not described. The objectives sounded formulaic and did not address how an adolescent with a significant tic disorder, severe obsessions, and many traumatic events could integrate these skills, improve his self-esteem, learn how to make friends, and transform his view of himself.

An army of consultants backed up the goals and objectives specified in the IEPs and primarily helped to focus the work of the case managers who were responsible for implementing Daniel's daily curriculum. Dr. Keefe, who had been a part of Daniel's life since elementary school, led the team which was comprised of Hester Brooks, EdD, who helped Daniel with his computer skills; Michael Cauley, PhD, a cognitive behavioral therapist; Bruce Masek, PhD, a behavioral medicine specialist at Children's Hospital; Daniel Brown, PhD, a psychotherapist; Edward Chapman, MD, his family doctor; Barry Fogel, MD, his neurologist; and Barbara Coffey, MD, a TS specialist. Each of these specialists helped Daniel in their area of expertise and contributed to his management, but his care remained poorly coordinated, and Daniel's course wildly fluctuated over these years.

The backbone of the homeschooling program remained behavioral management, but we eliminated punishing consequences. When Daniel became fidgety or his tics increased, his tutors would take a break or go for a walk. Like public school, the team assigned another area in our home as a time-out place near his "classroom" where he could discharge his tics. Although this worked at times, the team found that Daniel often needed to release energy by taking long walks or exercising. These adaptations were made under the auspices of a protection and containment policy agreed upon by our household and focused on issues such as inappropriate silliness and language, acting out, and "tic storms." The school district consultants anticipated that this would be good practice for Daniel's eventual inclusion back in school.

All Daniel wanted was to have a friend and be more like other kids his age; however, socialization was poorly integrated into his academic program. The damage done in elementary school festered, and he continued to lack confidence and self-esteem. Because he was so unlike boys his age, he missed being with other kids, spending most of his time around adults—case managers, caretakers, school personnel, healthcare personnel, and his family—which meant he had no chance to be a real teenager. The few homeschooling programs in the area we tried were in different suburbs and generally scheduled for only one hour; they were too brief and met inconsistently to achieve any of the stated goals. Their only benefit was that they broke up the daily monotony. We supplemented his school program with a social skills group led by Dr. Cauley, and Daniel finally made one friend who struggled with Asperger's Syndrome, talked nonstop about cars, and with whom he went bike riding regularly.

At the same time, to make up for his isolation, I tried to maintain some semblance of a "normal" family and arranged hikes, outings, visits with other relatives, and dinners at restaurants. We went on vacations to Vermont, New Mexico, Arizona, and Kentucky. Sometimes I had to bring a case manager to accommodate Daniel's restlessness and changing moods.

As if managing a team of six to ten people to educate and help my son, along with raising my other child and a full-time job weren't enough, to justify the necessity of homeschooling to the board of education, each year we were required to regularly apply and reapply to all the schools for special needs children in the wider Boston area. I always knew what was coming, but we had to complete a full application for each school, and each had different requirements which created reams of unnecessary paperwork. Each fall, I would visit five or six schools, accompanied by my lawyer, take a tour and discuss whether Daniel would fit into their programs. In general, the schools felt that they did not have the resources to meet his needs, often focusing on their inability to manage his tics. He was described by one of the school evaluators as "a youngster with neurological problems and periodic involuntary interpersonal space-invasive behavior. At times . . . unable to respond to verbal limits, and yet is traumatized, not reassured, by physical restraint." It seemed that it was preordained for every school to turn him down, but we had to repeat this humiliating ritual each September for three years. Although a tremendous waste of time and resources for both the schools and me, my hopelessness and sense of rejection gave me deeper insight into and empathy for how Daniel must have felt.

After three years of homeschooling, Dr. Keefe identified a program that would accept Daniel. We were cautiously hopeful! The team thought it would be helpful for him to be back in an environment where there were other kids, possibilities for socialization, and a more structured school day. I agreed and enrolled him in Pathways Academy, a school under the auspices of the Center for Neurointegrative Services at Boston's McLean Hospital. The school was developed in response to the needs of children and adolescents who were struggling or out of school. Programs were designed to meet the needs of children and adolescents whose cognitive abilities tended to be in the high average to superior range. At the time, their website promised, "The school's mission is to provide comprehensive services to a valuable at-risk population with developmental and neuro-integrative disabilities (e.g., Asperger's, TS) and to foster clinical and educational funding and research to extend and improve services" (McLean: Child & Teen Mental Health, 2025). Daniel fit the profile well and was accepted.

I attended Pathways Academy for almost two years from 1999 to 2001 and went to school from 9 a.m. to 2 p.m.. I was fourteen years old when I started. Pathways broke up the monotony of homeschooling. This program was on the grounds of a private mental hospital and had many buildings sprawling across a large campus. They did not give out high school diplomas. However, they were well-rounded in the subjects they were teaching, especially math and literature.

Only three students were enrolled. I stayed away from them and didn't make any friends. One of them was schizophrenic and the other had Asperger's and weighed over 340 lbs. But people were generally well behaved, and the environment was calm, with only occasional riots; the two other students would flip over the desks and barricade the doors. I stayed in my own corner of the room.

There were no punishments, restraints, or time out, and I was much freer. I would often go to the cafeteria for lunch. I would walk around the campus whenever I wanted on my own. It had beautiful scenery, and it felt very refreshing to walk around.

It wasn't like real school. The teachers taught subjects about forty minutes a day. The janitor and staff would teach us 'facts about life' as we learned what we could from them. For example, a staff member would sit on his desk and just talk about the importance of an education, discuss good hygiene, or teach us about how to budget money. At school they even set up a fish tank to make things more cheerful. I would read an occasional book. I often ran errands such as going to the gas station to pick up markers and pencils. Overall, I was often bored, and goofed around most of the day, but looking back on my experience I learned how to not be so reactive to the other student's provocations. I really learned a lot more of 'how to be' in life from my experience there.

Most of the teacher's reports, progress notes, and IEPs from this period suggest that Daniel was making progress, especially in academic areas where he received one-on-one supervision from a tutor. According to an assessment in 2001, he was more focused, able to concentrate, "more sensitive about his differentness," and eager to become involved with peers. Although there were many comments like this in the records, it seemed like double talk since the reports retracted them in subsequent comments. For example, after describing his eagerness to be involved with peers, this report went on to say that Daniel didn't know how to go about interacting with his classmates and was reluctant to take risks. Daniel remained shy and withdrawn, hung out at the edges of any group, and rarely initiated any contact with other children. He had little social experience and did not feel confident. He saw himself as a failure and was all too aware of the differences between himself and others.

I now better understand that one of the real values of routine schooling was learning the unwritten rules of socializing with other kids and in groups. The positive side of his exclusion was that Daniel maintained an innocence and sweetness that are often not apparent in more worldly kids.

In these reports, little was said about his tic disorder or his obsessions, which had worsened. Most importantly, they neglected to address Daniel's emergence into adolescence. During this time, he began to exercise more autonomy, which is developmentally on track, but this often took the form of resisting adult direction. His behavior became more unpredictable and, in some ways, even more worrisome. Despite the progress made in some areas, Daniel was becoming increasingly dejected and despairing about his life. Again, little mention was made of this in any of the reports or in the IEPs. Instead, the evaluators focused on increasing his independence, completing his homework, improving his written language and math skills, maintaining progress in reading comprehension, increasing his knowledge of US history, studying environmental science, and participating in community service—all important but ignoring his socialization and behavioral issues . . . and with dire consequences. In the winter of Daniel's first year at Pathways, he made a serious suicide attempt.

I awoke in the middle of the night to two burly police officers in my bedroom. Disoriented and startled, I asked them what they were doing in my home. Daniel had called 911 and told them he had overdosed but didn't want to die. I got dressed quickly and raced into Daniel's room. The EMTs had already moved him into the back of an ambulance in front of our house. Strangely, every surface I touched was sticky. When I got to the ambulance, Daniel said that he had poured honey over himself and everything around him because he wanted to "die a sweet death."

With sirens blaring, we arrived at the Children's Hospital ER, and Daniel was put into a room. The doctors drew blood. Daniel was groggy and uncommunicative. Initially, it was unclear what he had taken and whether he was becoming more unresponsive or whether he was going to metabolize some of the pills and improve. He fell into a deep sleep on a gurney, and I sat with him the rest of the night, not knowing what direction things were going. I was too afraid and frozen to call anyone until I was sure he was not going to die. I tried not to think about anything but just to make it through the night.

Fortunately, he began to improve and by morning was more awake. Because the hospital didn't have an available bed in the psychiatric ward, Daniel was sent to the cystic fibrosis unit for several days and placed on suicide watch with an aide. That caused another round of difficulties because Daniel guarded his privacy and didn't want anyone in the bathroom with him. He had frequent physical skirmishes with the aides until he was transferred to the psych unit where he said he did nothing except sit around. I remember no doctor consultations or family meetings aimed at processing Daniel's depression and despair or at understanding the events that led up to this young teen's suicide attempt. Again, it was all about management and goals but not the realities of his situation, his life.

When I was about fourteen or fifteen, I was depressed to the point where I felt like I was the saddest person on earth. I felt trapped. I felt like life had no pleasure. I wondered if all the bad things that happened to me were my fault. My voice was not heard. I did not understand how to ask for help. I did not understand how to cry for help. I was tired of life. I felt like I had already lived 100 years of hopeless misery. I had contemplated suicide for several months. I tried calling suicide hotlines, taking long walks, listening to depressing music. None of this helped. I eventually took a handful of Advil and Tylenol which would have killed me if I did not call 911. I called 911 because I changed my mind about dying. The ambulance came and I was given charcoal to swallow so that the Advil and Tylenol would pass through my system.

I awoke in a hospital and was confined within a room for 4 days. I was then transferred to a psych unit. I remained at the psych unit for two weeks. I complied. At the psych unit I felt the staff didn't care and were giving me trouble whenever they could. I did not get any constructive attention. The staff made fun of me and my choice of reggae music. I was terrified of the hospital

> *being like the movie One Flew Over the Cuckoo's Nest. This one wasn't but my later hospitalizations weren't far from that.*
>
> *When I got home, I felt even worse than I did before my suicide attempt. I felt powerless and weak. Nothing helped. It took two years for me to feel better again and by then I felt a million times better especially when I went back to high school and was around other people my age. I then left almost all of that in the dust. I will never forget how bad I felt or how stupid I was. I will never remember fully why I was that depressed but I think it came from a chemical imbalance in my brain coupled with how I was treated when I was eleven or twelve by poorly trained staff members in the old school I went to and how bored I was at home. I now know that suicide is never the answer. If only I knew then what I know now.*

Somehow, we made it through, Daniel came home, and we returned to a routine as best we could. During that time, yet another consultant commented on his adolescent behavior, saying:

> Daniel has become more like a typical teenager, but he has also been more reluctant to comply with directions. He is desperate to be more like his peers and is more aware of his differences. The lack of consequences and traditional interactions leads him to feel "Why bother?"
>
> I would characterize him as typically adolescent in most ways, but he is naïve and socially inexperienced.

She felt that he would benefit from being placed in a setting with other students since Daniel was a novice in social relationships. She also commented that as a youngster he had emotional outbursts that were of some concern, but now that picture was different as the TS tics were beginning to abate. Pathways was no longer an option. Since Daniel was of high school age, we enrolled him in Winthrop House, a public school near our home with a special program for troubled teenagers.

> Winthrop House, an off-site component of Brookline High School, provides a therapeutic Special Education alternative for students whose social and/or emotional problems has hindered success in a traditional setting. The goal of Winthrop House is to break the cycle of difficulties some adolescents

> experience in school. With its low student-teacher ratio, the program provides students individual support in an emotionally and physically safe environment, helping students build self-esteem, work toward academic potential, and experience positive peer interactions. (Public Schools of Brookline, 2025)

It all sounded good, but given our years of unhelpful and even traumatic experiences with the school system, I was cautious and prepared myself for the worst. After more than a decade of challenging experiences with the schools, it was hard to feel optimistic about the outcome. Winthrop initially emphasized focusing on social skills, the ability to make friends, study skills, writing, math, knowledge gaps, and anxiety during transitions between activities and home and school. Daniel's graduation date kept being moved to support his success, which required passing the Massachusetts Comprehensive Assessment System (MCAS) standardized tests. All through this, his vision was to "be a regular kid."

During the first semester at Winthrop, the staff was optimistic about Daniel's adjustment, yet shortly after, he was only able to tolerate two to three hours of class at a time. He made no friends and had trouble keeping up with the prescribed curriculum. He intermittently destroyed school property, especially in the bathroom. In fact, bathrooms anywhere (such as restaurants) became places Daniel invariably messed up by throwing things around, unrolling toilet paper, and occasionally urinating on the floor. To deal with his vandalism, the school kept him inside during lunch and breaks unless there was a staff person available to supervise him. He was not allowed on school grounds except during the limited hours designated in his plan.

During this time, one of his teachers wrote to me, "I'm confident given Dan's obvious intelligence and sensitivity that if he can persevere—that is, continue to muster the patience to deal with daily ups and downs—then he will achieve academic success." As his mother, who was not present during school hours, I wondered how they made comments like this that had so little correspondence to the reality of his situation.

> *Winthrop House was a place where I went during the day. It was just around the corner from the house I lived in and fortunately across the street from*

Starbucks. The other kids at the school were goth, punk, or gang members, as well as some other troubled kids. We would eat lunch at picnic tables and smoke cigarettes. The older kids would buy cigarettes for the younger kids. Nobody learned anything except how to act like a delinquent. The kids would bring knives to school. A thirteen-year-old kid pulled a knife on me after I poured a drink over his head. Later we got along because we played pool together at his house.

Generally, I felt ostracized by the other kids. The assistant teacher was a huge man with tattoos who would patrol the halls and check on us. The teachers would grade us however they felt like and I put almost no time into schoolwork. After a while I would only show up now and then and only stay for a short time. During the later years at Winthrop, I had two hospitalizations because of social neglect and unrelenting self-loathing due to my deteriorating mental state. I felt very depressed, and the voices began to appear, but at first no one knew about them. The environment made me feel very sad.

It is astonishing to me that although Daniel spent over three years at Winthrop, the school staff—the teachers, aides, and myriad specialists—remained unaware of Daniel's progressive decline. Many years later, Daniel told me it was during this time he started to hallucinate and hear voices, but none of the experts knew him well enough or were able to see him, *really* see him, and recognize the nature and depth of his difficulties and misery.

9

Boas, Fish, and Bees

Given his complicated life, we must ask, "Who is Daniel in all of this?"

He clearly had another side that became more prominent as he got older and took charge of his life. A wonderful therapist, one of the few, encouraged him to focus on who he was and to develop an authentic sense of self. As Daniel did, he began to understand that he was not just a label or a diagnosis or a bad person but had many strengths and admirable characteristics. However, it wasn't until he was in his thirties that he was able to develop enough self-confidence and sense of worth to feel good about himself and proud of how he had taken care of himself, various undesirable animals, and people in need.

Daniel has always been intensely interested in the natural world, especially slightly dangerous cold-blooded creatures like snakes and fish, as well as honeybees and insects—animals that most people ignore or are afraid of, not unlike him. He has become an expert on several species and cares for his "pets" with empathy and love. In the beginning, snakes were his favorites, and he collected giant ones that he tended to throughout childhood, adolescence, and beyond. Unfortunately, many people were terrified and would refuse to visit us, knowing we had a room full of giant snakes (all non-poisonous) living in enclosures in his bedroom.

> *I liked their markings and thought that they made phenomenally great pets because they are pretty, fun to watch as they crawled around, and were low-maintenance, although I had to adjust the heat and humidity in their*

enclosures. They would flip their tongues out to pick up small particles. I'm not afraid of them if they can't kill me and put me in the hospital.

Daniel was also an accomplished video gamer and, as a little boy, would sit in front of the computer screen with his favorite giant snake, "Kim," a red-tailed boa constrictor, draped over his shoulders. As she got bigger and stronger, we had to be more careful about Kim wrapping herself around Daniel's neck. In many ways, she served as a "transitional object" when Daniel was young, and he would walk around the house with her, feeling comfortable and safe when the snakes were with him.

On one occasion, Kim somehow escaped her enclosure and was "lost" for about six months. I spent many nights scouring the house to see if I could find her—fearing that she might be under my bed. I finally discovered her coiled in the bedsprings in a guest room. That's when I learned that snakes are like magicians and can slither under closed doors. They can also go into a state like hibernation and survive for extended periods without food. On another occasion, a small California banded king snake crawled down the bathroom sink drain and just stayed there, not moving in or out. We called the plumber, who removed the sink from its pedestal and put it into the bathtub until the snake finally crawled out weeks later and we could put the sink back together again. The snake was fine!

From my perspective, the biggest challenge was feeding the giant snakes. They ate live rats that Daniel had to care for if the snakes weren't hungry—especially since the rats were aggressive. It was hard to know when to feed them. As a single mom, helping Daniel care for the snakes became a source of pride for me. Occasionally, a rat bit Kim, and we would take the snake in a backpack to an "exotics" vet. To avoid infection, the snake needed antibiotics for two weeks that had to be administered intramuscularly. The vet taught me how to inject the snake underneath its scales. To solve the rat problem, we slowly weaned the snakes off live ones and began feeding them dead rats that we kept in a separate freezer in the basement.

Later, when Daniel lived in his own apartment, he had a ball python he named Sophia that he kept for seven years. When she died, Daniel grieved. Sophia was "big and strong, like a pit bull of a snake." Unlike boas, pythons are extremely muscular but usually only grow to five or six feet. He liked Sophia's temperament, especially her docility. He would take her out of the cage and allow her to crawl everywhere but had to be careful since he later adopted a little black cat. He finally gave up keeping snakes in the hope that it would make it easier to realize his wish of having a girlfriend.

As well as snakes, Daniel was enamored with fish. As a child, he had two tanks—a twenty-gallon one in his bedroom and a forty-gallon one downstairs in the foyer of our house.

It was very relaxing to watch the fish swim, and I enjoy caring for little creatures.

Daniel populated one tank with exotic and sometimes aggressive fish that could live in community together without a massacre. Occasionally, he misjudged, and we would find only skeletons floating on the water's surface. This always made Daniel very sad. As an adolescent, he upgraded to a seventy-five-gallon tank; he rescued a tattered old South American pacu fish that was going to be discarded by a pet store. Daniel nursed him back to health and was proud when he became so large that he was the only fish in his tank. Eventually, the fish got too big, and Daniel was sad when he had to return him to the pet store.

In addition to his love of snakes and fish, Daniel was attracted to bees from the time he was young. He would bring them into the house in plastic bags and scare everyone. With the help of a friend who was a professional beekeeper, he built two hives for Italian honeybees. Each hive held about 80,000 bees. They were very mellow and not aggressive. They tended to fly slowly and low, bringing pollen into the hive. He had a smoker that further slowed them down and calmed them. Although he had a protective suit, he didn't always wear it yet rarely got stung. With the help of our friend, he learned how the hives worked, where the queen lived, and most importantly, how to harvest honey. He collected many jars full and kept them in his bedroom closet. Over the years, the bees and hives were destroyed by mites and lack of adequate feeding at critical times. Even now, as an adult Daniel is still involved with beekeeping activities.

He was also drawn to creatures like scorpions and hissing cockroaches. When I found out the latter formed social communities and were being studied at Boston University, I surprised Daniel with one of them for his birthday, and he was thrilled. I did set a limit on having scorpions in the house—although disappointed, I think Daniel understood my fearfulness.

I did my best to nurture his interests, especially on family vacations. Both Daniel and I really enjoyed these times together. He loved seeing exotic animals in the wild, like in Arizona, where we climbed Camelback Mountain, and he was excited about finding an orange and black Gila monster, a type of lizard, and marveled at the swarms of bees flying by. These trips were a welcome refuge from the pressures at home. Because of Daniel's unpredictable behavior, I often invited one of the case managers on our trips, especially since my other child was with us and deserved my attention as well.

I remain amazed at Daniel's extensive knowledge and respect for all these creatures, his pleasure in working with them, and his tenacity in caring for them. It was easy to fully support these activities, although they were foreign to me and a little scary (especially the rats). I understood his connection to the natural world and his attraction to caring for these animals instead of playing baseball or engaging in other activities that young boys are involved with. His interests opened up a whole new and fascinating world to me. As a young adult, Daniel completed an online course and became certified as a herpetologist—a wonderful accomplishment.

Although Daniel had been raised in a house filled with golden retrievers, when it came to mammals, he preferred cats. As a young adult, he rescued a small black cat who weighed only six pounds from the shelter. Her name was Samantha. "She was a great cat and was home when I got there." As she aged, she developed kidney disease. Daniel hydrated her daily, put anti-nausea medicine in her ear flaps, and lovingly cared for her until she died after fifteen years. He recently rescued a large, aggressive white cat named Clara from a shelter; he was drawn to her story of abandonment by her elderly owner and chose her over other calm, sweet animals. Over time, with his superb caretaking, she has settled down and no longer attacks his feet or scratches him. She even cuddles with him on some nights. Daniel loves her and pays wonderful attention to all her needs. Clara has become his close friend and beloved companion.

Daniel developed many other interests. He was very athletic, excelling at individual sports such as skiing, snowboarding, and snowmobiling. From the time he was a young boy, he enjoyed martial arts. As an adult, he worked toward earning a black belt in karate. It is surprising that he can maintain the focused attention necessary to learn the complex mixture of moves. He is diligent about his class attendance and for years has gone three times a week—and even attended regularly online during the pandemic. He is also very musical. He plays the acoustic and electric guitar and has taken lessons for years. His teacher has commented that he is one of his most talented students. He likes all kinds of music and has a good relationship with his teacher.

I wonder what might have happened if the schools had been more aware of Daniel's special interests and wealth of knowledge about the natural world. They might have given him a way to support his self-esteem and build his confidence, especially with his classmates. Similarly, some of his caregivers and even the police might have viewed him more compassionately if they saw him as a growing boy with special interests. Instead, they only saw a frozen, troubled, naughty teen. In retrospect, as his parent, I too might have done more to highlight his interests and encourage his caregivers, doctors, and teachers to learn more about Daniel and his profound connection to the natural world.

10

What Did Daniel Have?

Daniel's many strengths were mixed with troubling and unpredictable behaviors. He was indeed a growing boy who was intrigued by nature, animals, and sports, yet his actions were often bizarre, out of control, erratic, and hard to understand. Undoubtedly, his childhood experiences helped to set the stage for what was to come. Daniel would often go for weeks behaving appropriately and seemed like any other "normal" young boy. But at random times it seemed, usually without warning, he would behave in very troublesome ways. Most kids ramp up before an explosive outburst, and there is some time to deescalate. Daniel would go from baseline to 100 in a matter of minutes and without any time to intercede. We received little help from our so-called helpers about how to contain these behaviors or even begin to understand and manage them.

One of the times I recall most vividly was when he was about six years old. I took him to the New England Aquarium because he loved watching the fish, especially the sharks, in the large central tank. As the aquarium became more crowded, I worried he might become overstimulated and decided we should go. As we descended to the ground floor, he grew increasingly agitated. We were standing quietly at the bottom of the tank about to leave when, for no obvious reason, Daniel punched me in the solar plexus with all his might. I landed on the ground, the wind knocked out of me, but mostly surprised. When asked why he did it, he had no answer.

This was minor compared to the outbursts that escalated as he got older. The episodes were frequent and troublesome, and most of the time we couldn't relate them to any specific precipitant. They just seemed to happen. Among the worst were when he destroyed a room in our house and everything in it—smashing furniture, throwing objects around, and tearing up books in a matter of minutes and without any apparent trigger.

As things deteriorated while he was still at school, he acted out in increasingly disturbing ways. As a young boy, he managed to talk the gas station attendant near our house into filling a milk container with gas. He brought it home and set fires on our tennis court emulating *Apocalypse Now* and incinerating the surface of the court. It was expensive and scary. When questioned about it, he narrated the plot of the movie.

> *After lighting the fires, I remember that the black burn marks on the tennis court were very visible. After seeing the size of the flames and realizing that they could be seen by people driving down the road I decided to do no more arson on the tennis court. I was very curious about fire. After lighting them I realized how dangerous it might be. My mom was upset and threatened to take me to a burn unit so I would learn the dangers of fire. I never lit another fire.*

Daniel broke glass regularly—mainly windows, but also glass tables and vases. Surprisingly, he never cut himself. I got to know all the glaziers in our area, and I always wondered what they thought because they never asked why we had so many broken windows. One cold Thanksgiving when my father was visiting, Daniel broke all the glass in a door that led to our garden. I hurriedly taped cardboard over the wreckage to avoid the inevitable lecture from my dad about how poorly behaved Daniel was and why I was unable to set better limits. I tried to help him understand by showing him videotapes about Tourette Syndrome, but he was resolute about my failure as a mom and critical of Daniel. He was traditional and from a different generation and never understood why I couldn't discipline my child.

Sadly, Daniel would impulsively smash his fish tanks with his barbells, and the fish would land on the floor, flapping around as they died. He was always heartbroken after one of these episodes because each fish had a name and was part of a community that he had taken great care to nurture. The tanks were large, and the water would drip through the light fixtures from the second to the first floor, requiring an electrician. Even after asking Daniel about what happened, he was unable or unwilling to say anything about why he demolished the tanks. But it was a regular occurrence. It would take Daniel months to regain his confidence and self-esteem after one of these episodes.

Further complicating this picture were Daniel's repeated skirmishes with the police. During his childhood and early adolescent years, he was charged with a range of crimes—none against people—all of which were eventually expunged. The police had little interest or knowledge of mental illness. The law was the law. Like my father, they were quick to blame and shame me for his behavior. How could I have raised a kid like Daniel? With the help of our lawyers, we did our best to shield Daniel from their animosity.

Some of his behavior was potentially dangerous—like his "sweet death" suicide attempt. We were fortunate he was never hurt. When Daniel was about ten years old, he mysteriously disappeared one evening, but not for long. Just after his return, all the lights in the town went out. Somehow, he had gotten into the town's central fuse box and defused the electrical system. Fortunately, they didn't catch the culprit who disconnected the wires, but it was a warning to us about his safety.

When Daniel was about fourteen years old, he was traveling on the subway and a group of boys his age was fooling around at the other end of the car. He got frightened about their intent and feared they might hurt him. He ran off the train in a panic as a police car inexplicably drove up. A young plainclothes officer wearing blue jeans jumped out. Daniel was unable to explain the sequence of events, but he felt terrified about his intent and got into a fistfight with the cop and was fortunately brought to the local hospital's ER rather than to jail. The police officer was understanding, called me, and connected me with the doctors to discuss Daniel's history. He was taking both Lamictal and Depakote at the time for presumed temporal lobe epilepsy, so after a long discussion and with my prompting they signed him out as having a seizure disorder. He was not charged with attempted assault but instead confined to his home for the next few months.

Some of his behavior was strangely amusing. Very early one morning when I was walking my dogs near his school, I noticed underwear taped to the lampposts. We'd recently gone on a trip to Times Square in New York City where Daniel had seen a Calvin Klein billboard of a man with six-pack abs advertising underwear and decided to replicate it at home.

When Daniel was an older adolescent, he got his driver's permit. He had been watching *Monty Python* and thought it would be amusing to change the direction of the flow of water from the windshield wipers of our car. On a hot summer day, he drove the car slowly on a busy street and soaked some of the vehicles and their passengers he passed. At about 11 p.m., the doorbell rang, and a law enforcement officer served notice of his arrest for "inciting road rage." Daniel had to appear before a magistrate. I called our lawyer, who accompanied us to court. Daniel dressed in the only suit he owned and sat frozen with fear, too frightened to move. The magistrate exhibited little understanding of mental health issues and lectured Daniel about his behavior. Daniel was so afraid that he was unresponsive. The magistrate interpreted his lack of affect and responsiveness as disinterest in the proceedings. She made it clear they usually fined people who received charges like these but felt that a fine only punished me. Instead, Daniel was mandated to community service—specifically serving dinner once a week for six months at a shelter for chronically alcoholic men. The magistrate didn't realize that although I was no stranger to shelters since I ran a national nonprofit for homeless families and children, this punished me far more than a fine since I had to drive him and support him through the dinners. The food was awful and even smelled bad, but Daniel interacted well with the men.

One of the most terrifying events put me on edge for years whenever we were in the car together. One spring day, Daniel and I were driving on Storrow Drive, a highway through Cambridge where the speed limit was around sixty mph. Daniel was in the back seat. Without warning, he reached up and pulled the emergency brake. The car spun out, and Daniel ran out of the car. After calming down, I felt only gratitude that we had not been killed. After that terrifying event, I always covered the emergency brake and tried to create a barrier between the front and back seats.

These episodes seemed unexplainable. As a psychiatrist, I turned to what I had learned early in my training: determining accurate diagnoses that could lead to management decisions that would help. For example, if a patient presents with a severe panic attack, the psychiatrist might consider prescribing low-dose Ativan, which would help initially but wouldn't lead to an understanding of what triggered the panic in the first place, so that the patient eventually might not need medication. Diagnoses, however, often precluded caretakers from trying to understand Daniel's daily experiences, strengths, and personhood, or appreciate the level of his distress and waning self-confidence. Most importantly, diagnoses did not necessarily tell us how best to address his difficulties. All they did was describe sets of symptoms over a specific period with no plan of action.

We were by far not the only ones to face these problems. Many books and articles have explored the psychiatric diagnostic system. In *Pathological: The True Story of Six Misdiagnoses* Sarah Fay researched the development of our current flawed system and illustrated through her own experience how its lack of scientific validity has been harmful, only increasing the bottom line for drug companies. In contrast to most medical diagnoses, psychiatric diagnoses—named but not explained in the Diagnostic and Statistical Manual of Mental Disorders (DSM)—are constellations of symptoms reported by patients or observed by clinicians for specified periods (American Psychiatric Association, 2013; Fay, 2022). As Dr. Thomas Insel, former director of NIH, described in his book, *Healing: Our Path from Mental Illness to Mental Health* psychiatric diagnoses have no specific tests, biomarkers, or laboratory tests to define them or guide us to effective treatments (Insel, 2022). When a diagnostic system is built on symptoms, its management focuses on symptom relief. It would be like treating chest pain caused by heart disease primarily with Tylenol. Insel emphasizes that the future of psychiatry, which might offer a path forward, includes genomics and neuroscience, but we are not there yet.

What the DSM manual does is provide doctors with a way of talking to each other about psychiatric problems and give insurance companies means to categorize patients. It provides a systematically codified and valuable common language written and updated by experienced researchers and clinicians from the highest echelons of academia and the scientific and medical communities, yet it has not been fully validated by scientific methods. Originally developed in 1952 by the American Psychological Association Committee on Nomenclature and Statistics, it has gone through many revisions—the latest leading to DSM-5-TR in 2022—a version that considers "the impact of racism and discrimination as well as culture, but still there is no consistent and direct correlation between labels . . . and effective treatment options" (American Psychiatric Association, 2013).

There are further limitations. As Dr. Herbert Pardes, former head of New York-Presbyterian Hospital, told Dr. Insel (2022), "When you tell me a patient has schizophrenia, you have told me maybe five percent of what I want to know about this person." Naming something doesn't fix it. It doesn't tell us about prevention, etiology, and treatment or the changing course of the disorder over time and how to manage its complicated progression. It doesn't tell us what the disability, disorder, or illness *means*. It doesn't explain the timeframes delimiting the disorders or the level of functioning that qualifies as a disorder. It doesn't explain the overlap of symptoms or what that means. It provides no guidance on how to treat a suffering mind, heart, or even soul—a human. It doesn't begin to describe the patient's internal felt experience. It also doesn't account for the person's hopes, wishes, and dreams. Most of all, it doesn't provide a roadmap for treatment, especially for the most serious disorders—schizophrenia and bipolar illness. Instead of helping patients, it gives us a way of further pathologizing them. As a surgeon, public health researcher, and Harvard Professor, Dr. Atul Gawande (2014) wrote in his book, *Being Mortal: Medicine and What Matters in the End*, "Medicine's focus is narrow. Medical professionals concentrate on the repair of health, not the sustenance of the soul" (p. 128).

Daniel's experience is an example of the shortcomings of a patient caught in a psychiatric diagnostic system that has minimal scientific validity and is unrelated to his inner experience or to treatment strategies. At one point, he met the criteria for twenty-two diagnoses that made little sense. In a way, it was understandable, though, since he had an array of complex symptoms and the DSM is an encyclopedia of symptoms, not a holistic consideration.

As a child, Daniel was consistently labeled with four diagnoses: attention deficit disorder with hyperactivity (ADHD), Tourette Syndrome (TS), obsessive-compulsive disorder (OCD), and temporal lobe epilepsy (TLE). I was convinced that he had both TS and OCD, which are often co-occurring disorders that meet DSM criteria. He may have had ADHD, but the symptoms are also present in many other disorders. The diagnosis of TLE is far more confusing given the variability of his MRI. Except for a single neurological test (a BEAM study), psychosis or schizophrenia was never really considered until Daniel was nineteen years old, even though my review of the school records and my experiences suggest he had a serious neurodevelopmental problem or psychosis far earlier.

Attention-Deficit/Hyperactivity Disorder (ADHD)

ADHD, the most diagnosed neurodevelopmental disorder in school-aged children, occurs in approximately 11 percent of American children aged four to seventeen years. In addition to inattention, the hallmark of ADHD, these children have trouble organizing and planning, following through on sustained tasks, completing assignments, and obeying the rules. Children who are hyperactive have trouble sitting still, are restless, and are on the move all the time. This constellation of symptoms often results in pervasive functional impairment, especially in a school setting, and certainly characterizes Daniel's behaviors, although they could also be explained by some of his other diagnoses (Dort et al., 2020; Ringer, 2019; Sayal et al., 2018).

Tourette Syndrome (TS)

Named for Gilles de la Tourette, this syndrome is a neurodevelopmental disorder characterized by sudden and repetitive motor and later phonic tics. It begins in early childhood with an estimated prevalence of 3-9/1000 children. The symptoms tend to peak by age ten to twelve, and then subside and disappear by late adolescence or early adulthood in approximately eighty to ninety percent of patients. This was Daniel's course. Its peak coincided with his expulsion from Manville at the age of eleven years and then disappeared fully by mid-adolescence. TS is often accompanied by various psychiatric disorders such as ADHD, OCD, and depression (Kleimaker et al., 2020).

Daniel had eye-blinking tics when he was about two and a half years old, and these progressed into multiple complex motor tics—such as neck jerking, hands flailing, dropping his pants, or acting aggressively. These behaviors were often accompanied by phonic tics in which he grunted, made strange noises, or yelled obscene phrases. In addition to the tics, individuals with TS suppress urges to perform a certain action for a short time, but this is followed by an increase in the tics. Daniel's tic disorder was poorly understood by the school staff, who often thought it was intentional and part of a behavioral problem, which led to his teachers being punitive and shaming (Centers for Disease Control and Prevention, 2024; Nani & Cavanna, 2019; Novotny et al., 2018). In retrospect I believe his TS was the primary reason he seemed unmanageable in elementary school.

Obsessive-Compulsive Disorder (OCD)

Approximately two to three percent or three million Americans have been diagnosed with obsessive-compulsive disorder (i.e., lifetime prevalence). The disorder usually begins early in life and persists well into adulthood, accounting for a large part of the global burden of disease. OCD is a genetic disorder characterized by obsessions that are intrusive, unwanted, anxiety-laden, distressing thoughts, worries, images, and urges that are generally unrealistic (Lochner et al., 2005; Stein et al., 2019).

Compulsions are repetitive behaviors a person feels forced to perform to reduce the distress and feared consequences often following a set of rigid rules. They are in response to obsessions. According to the DSM-5, obsessions or compulsions may occupy more than an hour a day and are so distressing that they interfere with important areas of functioning. OCD commonly co-occurs with anxiety disorders, mood disorders, substance abuse, and tic disorders.

Daniel's obsessions and compulsions are like those described in many community and patient samples. He has had OCD most of his life, and it remains an active problem. His most disturbing OCD symptoms are related to personal cleanliness. I became aware of his OCD when he was eight years old. I had a cold, and Daniel insisted I wash everything I touched, including clothes, doorknobs, and dishes. I remember spending an inordinate amount of time washing clothes until it dawned on me that I was dealing with OCD. He still often showers multiple times a day with at least three different soaps and changes his clothes frequently. He won't wear a shirt more than once and will change and wash his blue jeans daily. In a single week, he may wear as many as thirteen different shirts. His laundry loads are enormous. The other side of this disorder is his messy but generally clean apartment—usually cluttered with unwashed dishes in both the kitchen and living room, as well as papers strewn around.

As an adult, Daniel's OCD often interferes with his functioning. When he leaves his apartment, he takes an inordinate amount of time to get from the front door because he has various rituals that take considerable time, such as checking everything in his apartment before going anywhere, and as a result, he's often late.

Temporal Lobe Epilepsy (TLE)

"Epilepsy is the most common chronic brain disease and affects people of all ages. More than 50 million people worldwide have epilepsy" (World Health Organization, 2025). However, less than one-third of people with epilepsy have adequate control of their seizure disorder. TLE was included in the epilepsy classification in 1989 and is a localized disorder; the temporal lobe is the area of the brain most capable of generating seizures (Téllez-Zenteno & Hernández-Ronquillo, 2012). The most common cause is sclerosis of the area of the brain called the hippocampus. "The most common clinical pattern is lack of responsiveness and staring, often accompanied by hand and mouth automatisms (e.g., lip smacking, swallowing, or chewing movements)" (Téllez-Zenteno & Hernández-Ronquillo, 2012). Patients with epilepsy have an eightfold higher risk of having an accompanying psychosis, and the rate is even higher in TLE. The psychosis of TLE, I discovered, was hard to treat and tended to be persistent and troublesome.

When Daniel was about fourteen years old, he was seen by a neurologist who was certain he had TLE and referred him to one of the experts in Boston. At that time, his MRI and EEG suggested that he had a "signature lesion" in his temporal lobe which can manifest like schizophrenia. Interestingly, a TLE expert I consulted told me that Daniel's propensity for breaking glass was likely associated with TLE.

Dr. Fogel, the Harvard neurology professor who was the first to diagnose Daniel with TLE, put him on a panoply of drugs for seizures including Lamictal, then Tegretol, Campral from overseas, huperzine, and modafinil to counteract his sleepiness. Lamictal can cause a rash, which Daniel developed. It may indicate the beginning of Stevens-Johnson syndrome, a potentially lethal side effect, so we stopped the drug. It's hard to know if these drugs did anything helpful since nothing seemed to change except that he complained of being sleepier. Daniel was then referred to one of the TLE experts in Boston, who affirmed his diagnosis of TLE. He saw him intermittently for about three years.

Daniel's repeated and recent MRIs and EEGs have been completely normal, raising the question of the veracity of the diagnosis. It's possible that the TLE diagnosis partly explained his unpredictable sudden outbursts and later his psychotic behavior. Although I had initially deferred to my colleagues, I remained skeptical enough to agree to discontinue his seizure medication regimen (Blair, 2012; Elliott et al., 2009). It didn't seem to make any difference. At this point in our lives, little did.

Post-Traumatic Stress Disorder (PTSD)

The primary importance of trauma in the development of mental illness was not fully recognized until the 1990s and after—when Daniel was already in his twenties. Thus, it is not surprising that it did not appear in Daniel's records or testing. Although he was never labeled with PTSD, I wondered how much of his mental illness was a manifestation of severe cumulative stresses that included his early childhood experiences as well as his interactions with the schools, his teachers, many of his so-called helpers, and his peers, as well as the psychotic illness itself and the myriad hospitalizations. From the loss of his birth mother and Rachel, to the arrival of the other birth mother, his father's and my divorce, his run-ins with the police, our house fire, his expulsion from Montessori and then summer camp, to his multiple chaotic transfers from one school to another—all culminating in his experience at Manville where he was repeatedly ill-treated; he was traumatized—a setup for developing PTSD (Herman, 2022, 2023; Moskowitz et al., 2019; Mueser et al., 2009; Patel et al., 2014; van der Kolk, 2015).

It's possible his PTSD reached an extreme. Perspectives on severe psychopathology are evolving, especially regarding the relationship among trauma, dissociation, and psychosis. Particular attention has focused on the presence of psychotic symptoms in dissociative disorders and dissociation among patients with schizophrenia. For example, many patients labeled with dissociative identity disorder (DID) report hearing voices but are generally not delusional or have thought projection—distinguishing them from schizophrenia (Moskowitz et al., 2019).

As our understanding of how healing occurs in trauma and its impact on the brain, mind, body, and soul has evolved, so have our interventions proliferated—it seems far more than in other branches of medicine (van der Kolk, 2015). I can't help but wonder if we had known more about some of these strategies early on in Daniel's life that we might have used them to help him manage his unusual experiences. Perhaps we might have changed his downhill course.

Schizophrenia

Schizophrenia is a common, chronic, and often serious mental illness. "It is a mental disorder characterized by disruptions in thought processes, perceptions, emotional responsiveness, and social interactions" (National Institute of Mental Health, n.d.). It is one of the top fifteen causes of disability worldwide, and estimates of the prevalence of schizophrenia and related psychotic disorders in the US range between 0.25 percent and 0.64 percent, or 3 million adult individuals annually (National Institute of Mental Health, n.d.). The prevalence based on claims analysis is 5.1 per 1000 lives annually (Wu et al., 2006). In both my professional and personal experience, I learned that the illness is characterized by positive symptoms such as hallucinations and delusions, as well as negative and cognitive symptoms such as social withdrawal, amotivation, interference with working memory, and decreased processing speed. Daniel developed most of these symptoms by late adolescence.

Esmé Wang, in her collection of essays about her experience with mental illness and that of others, describes schizophrenia as follows:

> Schizophrenia terrifies. It is the archetypal disorder of lunacy. Craziness scares us because we are creatures who long for structure and sense. . . . We hope for ways to corral and control bad fortune, illness, unhappiness,

> discomfort, and death—all inevitable outcomes that we pretend are anything but. And still, the fight against entropy seems wildly futile in the face of schizophrenia, which shirks reality in favor of its own internal logic. (Wang, 2019, p. 3)

When Daniel was hospitalized in 2004, he was diagnosed with schizophrenia for the first time. I was resistant and terrified of this label, yet the diagnosis mattered since it had significant implications for choosing medications that might be helpful. I went to visit him on the first day he was hospitalized. He was agitated, pacing, and disheveled. He looked a wreck and kept insisting I get the staff to turn off the loud music . . . but I didn't hear any music. That's when I realized he was psychotic; my fear of a schizophrenia diagnosis was about to be realized. As both a mother and a psychiatrist, it was a startling, disturbing, and unforgettable moment.

During this time, Daniel was internally preoccupied, disorganized, unable to function, and had difficulty communicating. He was acting bizarrely, fidgety, and sometimes aggressive. His personal hygiene was terrible, and he had trouble dressing himself. He paced around the ward with no shoes, moving erratically. He slept on a plastic mattress and was withdrawn yet simultaneously restless. He was unable to follow directions on the psychiatric unit where he was hospitalized, so the staff either put him in a room by himself or required that he stay in bed. The various medications they gave him didn't seem to help, so they kept adding more drugs until he was on multiple neuroleptics—antipsychotic medications. He did not have a gradual or adequate trial period for a single medication. When he became more agitated, they used Benadryl to settle him down. These drugs did not seem to be used to treat him but rather to sedate him and stop the difficult behaviors.

While Daniel was hospitalized, he paced around the ward, uncommunicative and not making much sense. He was in the thrall of his auditory, visual, and kinesthetic hallucinations and often delusional—worried that people were going to poison or hurt him. Most characteristic of the auditory hallucinations in acute schizophrenia is the description by Lori Schiller in her book *The Quiet Room*.

> They popped up when I least expected them. Occasionally they were friendly, but mostly they reviled me, shouting in their hoarse, harsh tones: "You must die, you bitch," they shrieked. "Die! Die! Die!" . . . I was always afraid that I was going to die, because that's what the Voices said would be my fate. . . . When the Voices began to screech and cackle, I looked to the floor. Sometimes I held my breath, hoping, somehow, to outlast them. . . . What tortured me more than anything was when the Voices laughed at me. It was a kind of a hysterical laughter, as if I was the target of everyone's jokes. I didn't know why they were making fun of me so viciously, but I hated myself for being the sitting duck for ridicule. (Schiller & Benett, 1996, pp. 21–2)

As I came to see, the characteristics of Daniel's hallucinations changed significantly as his illness unfolded. When he was first hospitalized, they were threatening—similar to Schiller's description (Schiller & Bennet, 1996). Over time they ranged from harassing and vicious to some voices that were friendly and kind. At times, they made him laugh and were companionable and entertaining, while at other times, they harassed him or even threatened his life. His voices were primarily auditory and visual, but occasionally kinesthetic—he could feel them.

Contrary to popular opinion, auditory hallucinations are not pathognomonic of schizophrenia and may be present in 1–3 percent of the general population (Waters & Fernyhough, 2017). In fact, many people who hear voices do not suffer from mental illness at all. No single feature of hallucinations, apart from age of onset in late adolescence, indicates a diagnosis of schizophrenia. Many aspects of hallucinations are present in other psychiatric disorders, medical and neurological conditions, substance use disorders, and, most important, non-clinical groups (Turkington et al., 2016). Oliver Sacks, in his book *Hallucinations,* surprisingly does not include a discussion of schizophrenia, stating that these "demand a separate consideration, a book of their own" (2013), however, he describes an array of disorders in which hallucinations are a major feature and emphasizes how many cultures associate them with religious practices and spirits. Sacks wondered "to what extent hallucinatory experiences have given rise to our art, folklore, and even religion" (Sacks,

2013, p. xii). In his view, "Hallucination is a unique and special category of consciousness and mental life" (Sacks, 2013, p. xiii).

According to the DSM, a diagnosis of schizophrenia may be associated with auditory and visual hallucinations but assumes the presence of concurrent symptoms. These include delusions, disorganized speech, grossly disorganized behaviors, and negative and cognitive symptoms (e.g., lack of motivation, decreased emotional expression). From DSM-III in 1980 to DSM-5 in 2013, the diagnosis of schizophrenia included some subtle changes in its view of hallucinations. In 1980, hallucinations were elaborately described and considered along with delusions as essential for the diagnosis. Voices had to be present for more than a few moments. In contrast, in 2013, either delusions or hallucinations or disorganized speech had to be present, and hallucinations were not specifically described.

Specifically, DSM-5 (Substance Abuse and Mental Health Services Administration, 2016)[1] describes schizophrenia (295.90) as "Two (or more) of the following, each present for a significant portion of time during a 1-month period (or less if successfully treated). At least one of these must be (1), (2), or (3):

1. delusions
2. hallucinations
3. disorganized speech (e.g., frequent derailment or incoherence)
4. grossly disorganized or catatonic behavior
5. negative symptoms (i.e., diminished emotional expression or avolition)."

Going on to say:

> "For a significant portion of the time since the onset of the disturbance, the level of functioning in one or more major areas, such as work, interpersonal relations, or self-care, is markedly below the level achieved prior to the onset (or when the onset is in childhood or adolescence, there is failure

[1]Author's note: There were a few significant changes in DSM-5-TR.

to achieve the expected level of interpersonal, academic, or occupational functioning)."

And:

"Continuous signs of the disturbance persist for at least six months."

Daniel at various times in his long illness had many of these features but also had visual, auditory, and kinesthetic hallucinations that varied in intensity, viciousness, and impact on his functioning—and changed over the many years he was so ill (McCutcheon et al., 2020). Even now he must manage the voices that are intermittently present in his life, but he has learned various ways of living with them.

Although Daniel met the criteria specified in DSM-5 for schizophrenia, the change reflects an expanding understanding of hallucinations. There is emerging literature that suggests they may be a psychological response to stressors and exposure to adversity and trauma, given the lack of specific biomarkers (Galińska-Skok & Waszkiewicz, 2022). Some have questioned the diagnosis itself.

The phenomenological similarities in voice hearing among different subgroups and their relationship to a range of stressors have helped strengthen the contention that voice hearing may be more reliably associated with psychosocial and cultural variables rather than specific clinical diagnoses. It raises many questions about the relationship to trauma and adverse childhood experiences, especially Dissociative Disorders in which people experience distinct parts or identities—parallel to distinct voices—and complex PTSD (Fisher, 2017; Longden, 2017).

If you hear voices, you might hear ten voices and eight of them might be bad and making stuff up, torturing you. They might say things like, "Oh, you're going to have cancer in three days if you don't throw out every pack of oatmeal you have" or whatever. I'm just trying to say that you might have two voices that are good, and you might as well focus on the voices that are good if you can, rather than bad ones because they will unrelentingly torture you all day long. And this book is going to help a lot of people as to what it's like having schizophrenia so they can be more understanding and there will be less stigma surrounding even having schizophrenia.

The stigma is that people are going to judge you. They're going to think, "Oh, he's a freak-o. He needs to take a pill right now." Or "Oh, he's not going to work for me. He's a liability." It's stigma.

When the first doctor gave me the label of schizophrenic, I thought the rest of my life was over...it really ended part of my life.

Do These Labels Matter?

Regardless of the diagnosis or combination of diagnoses, and with the exception of medication choices, labeling all led down the same road; the diagnoses were not combined with specific treatment recommendations, but the catalog of symptoms all suggested the need for establishing connections to other people and compassionate trusting therapeutic relationships, behavioral strategies that helped manage the symptoms when necessary, and mobilization of robust supports.

As I came to see, what was repeatedly left out of the diagnostic equation was seeing Daniel as a whole person with hopes, wishes, and dreams, but with symptoms that required management that were only a small part of who he was. No one is solely their illness, and most of all, Daniel, who is now an adult with complex experiences in the world, is driven by his mind, heart, and soul. We should recall Hippocrates' often-quoted words: "It is more important to know what sort of person a disease has than to know what sort of disease a person has."

If teachers and diagnosing clinicians had been able to see Daniel wholly, had known what sort of person he was, would his road still have been downhill leading to florid psychosis? We'll never know, but what we do know is that we need to learn more about how the brain works and to better understand the experiences and perceptions of patients.

11

Reign of Terror

According to the hospital records, in 2001, Daniel was admitted for two weeks to McLean Psychiatric Hospital for "behavioral dyscontrol." We remember most of his admissions, but this one—like much of his teenage years—eludes both Daniel and me. It seemed yet another part of the general downhill course we traveled, but represented the beginning of a long, terrifying, and discouraging course that felt unrelenting.

I do, however, recall with cinematic clarity the events of early 2003 when Daniel, who was nineteen years old, was again admitted to McLean for several weeks for "bipolar and psychotic disorders" and worsening behavioral dyscontrol. He had become increasingly destructive at home (but never hurting anyone)—precipitously smashing furniture, throwing barbells through his fish tank, and breaking windows—culminating in a four-hour siege that has been seared into my memory.

Earlier that day, Daniel had visited a residential facility not far from where we lived called Eikos that he seemed interested in attending, a setting his treatment team and I thought would benefit him. However, this meant leaving our home where he had grown up and beginning his separation from me, his mom. Despite our complicated relationship and his attempts at independence, he was attached to me; I was his anchor, defender, and safe harbor, so he was intensely fearful. After all, he had been mostly homeschooled since the fifth grade and had little experience socializing or being in other settings, and his confidence and self-esteem were at a low point.

Daniel's behavior after the visit to Eikos remains one of the worst nights of my life. I still have flashbacks and a visceral response whenever I think about what happened and how it set off a cascade of frightening and awful events. That evening, Daniel took two large butcher knives from the kitchen and began a four-hour rampage in which he indiscriminately destroyed anything in his path. Over the evening, Daniel cut up my chairs, smashed furniture, slashed my computer screen, sliced up my books and plants, kicked the dogs he loved, and superficially cut his palms and smeared blood all over the walls. He refused to put down the knives. Over time, he become increasingly agitated and scary.

Although he was a young man almost six feet tall and 170 pounds and nearly twice my size, I believed, perhaps erroneously, that he wouldn't hurt me. It was a terrifying siege that went on for hours, but I was resolute about not calling the police since I feared they might shoot him. I telephoned his father, who was unavailable, and finally, not knowing what else to do, I put on several of my down-filled ski jackets and pairs of gloves, assuming that he couldn't cut through so much fabric with any speed. I cornered him at a turn on our narrow back staircase, firmly told him to drop the knives and go sit in the den and not move. Fortunately, unpredictably, and thankfully, he followed my directions.

I sat with him for a few minutes saying nothing and then told him we had to go to the hospital. We were both exhausted and depleted from the rampage. I called McLean, and since he had a few small cuts on his hand, they insisted he be medically cleared at an emergency room near us before psychiatric admission. I tried my best to talk them out of this, but they were resolute. Given his mental state, the hospital (as usual) was following protocol and ignoring our immediate needs. So, we left the house.

I was afraid he might do something dangerous in the car. This concern was not unfounded after what we'd experienced when he commandeered the emergency brake on Storrow Drive, yet I had no choice. I insisted he sit in the back seat and barricaded the divide between us.

Daniel was extremely agitated when we arrived at the local ER, and they were slow to see him; there was no way we could wait, and since the scratches on his hands weren't serious, I signed out against medical advice, told him to get back into the car, and sped to McLean where they readily admitted him. I was so relieved that my son was in a safe place, and we were all unharmed. Even now, when I think about that night, I feel fear, extreme concern about Daniel, and overwhelming sorrow for all of us and for the lack of support. Being alone in this situation heightened my terror as I became increasingly aware of how out of control Daniel was and how sick he had become despite more than a decade of efforts to understand and treat his bizarre and scary behaviors.

The attending psychiatrist at McLean described his view of Daniel's relationship with me in the hospital records. These highlight the discrepancy between their perspective and mine. The hospital notes I have from that period state that Daniel exhibited "remarkably complex and sadistic behavior toward his mother just prior to admission during which time he cut up her plants, beat her dog, came after her with butcher knives, managed to cut himself and smear blood all over the walls, slashed her computer screen, having recently urinated in her food and placed dog food in her bed."

In the same set of notes, Dr. A. commented on how dangerous Daniel seemed to have become and worried I was minimizing the threat. Dr. A. wrote:

> This was a common misperception (e.g., that mothers can handle their children) in relationships such as this and was often the misperception of the female member before she was seriously harmed. In addition to the episode, just prior to his hospitalization he had taken some lighter fluid, placed it in bottles, lit them on fire and threw them out of the windows while she was having dinner guests. Everyone ran outside to put the fire out and Daniel locked them out of the house.

Daniel told the doctors, "I just wanted to offend her so much that she would never speak to me again. I know it would be good for me to not have her so much in my life, although I know she is my mom." Dr. A. was pessimistic about being able to work out the "psychotic transference" to me during this hospitalization, especially given Daniel's long history of numerous therapists and extensive treatments. Daniel later told me that Dr. A. called him "a monster who should be locked up in a cold, dark cell all day."

Notwithstanding what to me appeared to be blatantly psychotic behavior, Daniel was discharged with a diagnosis of "impulse disorder NOS" (not otherwise specified), history of ADHD with marked antisocial features, history of limbic temporal dyscontrol, and temporal lobe epilepsy. *There was no mention of psychosis or schizophrenia.* These labels were not helpful, and at discharge, he was taking Lamictal, Depakote, Keppra, Seroquel, and Ativan together; yet this mixture only sedated him.

Daniel denied delusions and hallucinations, but was paranoid, internally preoccupied, and his insight and judgment were poor. He was scary and uncommunicative. During this period, and after he calmed down in the hospital, Dr. A. insisted Daniel was a danger to me. It is only in retrospect that it became clear my son's disorganization was partly due to the suggestion of separation from me and our home—an enormous milestone in his life. At the time, we were unable to deal with this directly, which left Daniel with many feelings that he acted out and which I didn't pick up on, overwhelmed as I was by the whirlwind of disorganization. At that point, I had little energy for more than staying entirely focused on keeping everyone safe.

At the suggestion of McLean Hospital, we made plans to have Daniel admitted to Eikos, the Boston residential therapeutic community he had toured. We thought this might help him settle down given the structure and rules and give him a chance to connect with peers and, most importantly, begin the painful process of separation.

> EIKOS serves clients 25 years and older with major psychiatric diagnoses: schizophrenia, schizoaffective, bipolar, or anxiety disorders; and major depression. In addition, we serve adults with varied psycho-social profiles who need a safe, therapeutic transition to greater health and independence....
>
> The name "EIKOS" is derived from the Greek word OIKOS which means "home, household or extended family community."

Daniel moved into Eikos and was assigned a private room with a shared bathroom in one of the houses near the main building where the community dayroom was located. He lived there for about a year and a half. Daniel summarized his experience at Eikos as "Okay because no one beat me up or bothered me." What he remembers most about the time is the restaurants where he and the other residents ate. He would sometimes attend a support group where participants were urged to talk about relationships and community issues, but he did not find them useful and participated minimally. He remained uncommunicative and withdrawn and didn't share his internal preoccupations with anyone. No one was aware that he was hearing voices that were partially dictating his behavior.

Daniel recalls various people at Eikos but characterizes them as troubled and a few as "too crazy." Although he spent a lot of time alone in his room playing video games on a computer, he found some peers that he hung out with and also became involved with a nearby encampment of homeless people, many of whom he joined in the mornings to drink Steel Reserve and Magic Hat beer.

I did not see him as often as I would have wished while he was at Eikos because he wished to be more independent, but with that independence came a whole new set of companions.

> *When the voices first came into my head, I was forced to hear them all day long and I remember thinking, "How do the voices find the time to be present and talk to me all day?"*

12

A Community of Spirits

Daniel crossed over into a parallel reality inhabited by an ever-expanding chorus of voices—some friendly, some terrifying. Sadly, his deterioration was not apparent to the Eikos staff, or if it was, they were at a loss to know how to address it. As these voices materialized, each had a distinct personality and a name. They seemed to have specific functions that might represent part of Daniel's psyche and experience. As the voices multiplied, Daniel became more psychotic and out of contact with reality.

Some of the speakers were transparent, and he could see through them, "kind of like a poltergeist." Others impersonated famous people.

> *It's like if you put a poster on the wall and then you took a slide projector and projected an image on it, you would see the image from the slide projector, but you would also see the image of the poster behind it. It's like that . . . What they would do is get in the way of me closing and opening doors and things like that. And it would look like they were there, so I might not close the door, and I would wait until they moved.*

He did not share the specifics of his experience with anyone until recently because the denizens of his mind interfered with his ability to function or relate to people, and he was unwilling to describe them in any detail. As he has recovered from the ravages of his illness, he has learned to navigate between both worlds. The descriptions that follow here are based on our recorded conversations almost twenty years after Daniel's initial hospitalization. It was the first time he talked openly about his internal life and seemed eager to describe the characteristics of each voice in detail. His willingness to do this reflected how much he has grown.

> *The way the voices are makes me wonder if they're some kind of spirits. The other explanation is my brain misfiring. Or it could be even mixture of both of those. Either way, they're not going to give me the trouble I used to get from them, I don't mind hearing voices at all. In fact, I might even get bored if I didn't have them around these days. Pretty bored.*

Through our many conversations, Daniel allowed me to enter his alternate reality in part because his illness has eased and many of the voices have retreated, become quieter, and even friendly, assuming different roles while retaining the same general characteristics. Now, over two decades later, Daniel objectively describes how he can hear, see, and feel his "community of spirits."

As he began to share his parallel world, I came to better understand my son in a way his myriad doctors and mental health providers never could. They were experts, some of the best in the country, and as I've described, provided plenty of labels, diagnoses, and treatment plans, but missed the individual, person-to-person exploration of his illness, or a real understanding of his unusual perceptions and experiences of the world and people around him. To transcend the labeling that went on for years and didn't adequately capture or connect with Daniel's nature, I hired a graphic designer to draw the spirits. Daniel was able to email the illustrator a short paragraph of precise details about each voice so that the artist could easily render them in black and white, and then, with a few minor corrections from Daniel, complete them in color. It was a surprisingly brief process, and the result was unexpected. The drawings are beautifully imaginative and, to Daniel, unwaveringly real.

Although medical and popular literature is replete with descriptions, studies, and even first-person accounts and memoirs about schizophrenia and related common disorders, they are surprisingly lacking in their attention to the landscape and texture of worlds like the one Daniel lives in. Most clinicians are focused on the nature of a patient's symptoms rather than understanding their experience, impact, and the complexity of their reality and how it operates. The DSM describes the disorders and their timeframes for the purpose of determining and systematizing diagnostic criteria (American Psychiatric

Figure 12.1 *Diesel, The Bishop, and The Sheriff.*

Association, 2013). Along with an increasing focus on neuroscience, these perspectives dictate views of these highly stigmatized and devastating disorders but do little to fully understand them.

Daniel's voices are auditory, visual, and unusually, kinesthetic. As he puts it,

> *I see them floating nearby, walking around, and sometimes they show up in little TV screens that seem to pop out of my eye. I also hear them talking among themselves and to me. Several of the more malicious voices try to touch me provocatively and I can feel them; when they do this, I have trouble functioning and try to stop them.*

Hallucinations are not pathognomonic of schizophrenia but are a common symptom of this serious disorder. Auditory and visual hallucinations also occur in other psychiatric conditions, neurodegenerative diseases like Parkinson's and dementia, and other sensory disorders, drug and alcohol conditions, and (according to Oliver Sacks) in people with no obvious clinical problems (Sacks, 2013). Recent literature also suggests that post-traumatic experiences may shape the nature of the hallucinations, and that voice phenomenology may mirror experiences from the past (van den Berg et al., 2023). Hallucinations take different forms and are interpreted differently in diverse cultures and religions (Lukoff, 1985; Ragins, 2021; Van Ysslestyne, 2018). Some equate them to the experiences of indigenous shamans and other spiritual groups and question their relationship to mythic and otherworldly realms, "perhaps a vehicle for something profound," as Dick Russell described in such a compelling way in his memoir *My Mysterious Son* (Russell, 2018). Others from Carl Jung to Teresa of Ávila, Ramakrishna to Emanuel Swedenborg, have described mystical experiences that have psychotic features and appear similar to the symptoms of schizophrenia as well (Coward, 1979; Fittipaldi, 1989; Jones & Fernyhough, 2008; Kakar, 1992).

> *Some people are in tune with the spirit world. They can see things that are in the aerial realm around them, like people floating around connected to white cords and stuff. And I've seen a lot of that. I don't know what the white cords are, but I've seen The Sheriff floating in the aerial realm with the cord connected to him. And I've seen some of The Bishop's monks come out of the bishop and float around me and they were connected to a white cord. I believe the white cord connects you to the body of the person that is astral traveling.*
>
> *I'm either in tune with spirits or it's my brain misfiring. It's one or the other. It seems very spiritual and that might be in my head and spirits from beyond. People-like spirits that died but they didn't move onward to heaven or purgatory. Instead, they stayed in this realm because they were unable to leave because of a certain attachment. So, they would take it upon themselves to haunt me. That's one explanation. But the other explanation is my brain. It could be a mixture of both of those. And there's no other explanation. Those two explanations, that's my belief.*

At first the voices talked to each other constantly, telling and retelling the same stories and then rearranging the order in which they told the stories. The conversation became a "big circle," repeating the same things month after month. At first, Daniel listened intently and then figured out how to ignore them when he realized their stories were recurring and circular. Sometimes the chatter was so loud he would try to block them out by any means available: putting on headphones, turning up the volume on his TV, or running the water in his bathtub.

The voices occasionally spoke to Daniel directly and still do, asking questions like: *What are we going to do about Daniel? How long do we have to talk to Daniel? When is Daniel going to get it?* They often make up stories about past lifetimes but, as he puts it, "I don't pay attention to any of it because they can go on forever." Much of the time the voices ask Daniel not to talk and get angry if he says anything vulgar.

Sometimes the spirits pop out of his body, yell something, and then pop back in. They also act as impersonators and imitate celebrities from television shows, movies, rock bands, and the news. Some of their favorites in the past have been Rodney Dangerfield, Stephen Colbert, Midnight Oil Band, William Shatner, Adam Sandler, Sheryl Crowe, and Taylor Swift. They also impersonate people from cartoons. More recently, they have asked Daniel not to listen to so many metal bands and will say things to him like, "We don't want you listening to Motorhead, Alice Cooper, or Marilyn Manson. Listen to Twisted Sister or to Bon Jovi."

> *If I'm not vulgar and I don't talk to them much and I listen to just the right music, they really leave me alone. If I don't, then they come and they tell me that I'm going off the deep end and they're trying to stop me from going off the deep end. Which is fine, by the way.*

Daniel was nineteen years old and sitting in the community dayroom at Eikos when he first saw Diesel out of the corner of his vision. He was not startled or alarmed by her presence and thought "*Whatever. . .*" Diesel is an easygoing thirty-year-old muscular, bald, large-breasted, attractive woman who wears a black corset, blue jeans, and tall leather boots. She lives in Hell's Kitchen in New York City where she owns a jewelry store that Daniel has visited in his imagination. She calls him "Dear," not Daniel, and mediates among the other voices giving helpful advice like asking them to grill sausages for Daniel. When the other voices argue among themselves, Diesel whispers calming words to reduce Daniel's tension. She has been his companion and protector for over two decades. He likes it when she shows up and still misses her if he doesn't see her regularly. Daniel says it's "a plus having her as a voice."

After the appearance of Diesel, a succession of voices emerged over the next weeks at Eikos: The Fat Man, the Sheriff, TJ, the Pimp, and William. The Fat Man is "exactly that"—very fat. Diesel is good friends with the Fat Man, and they often engage in chatty conversations. The Fat Man constantly says "exactly that," but Daniel doesn't really know what it means. He weighs five hundred pounds but can still walk. He is about fifty years old, always wears a brown

Figure 12.2 *Diesel.*

T-shirt, and hangs around Diesel. He always carries a glass bottle that he hits people with. He drinks too much. When he went to prison, he was allowed to keep the bottle but broke it after he bashed someone on the head. He lived on the streets for a while but didn't have a bottle at that time. Daniel viewed him as "a cool voice" because he never annoyed him.

The Fat Man feels that "life isn't fair" and doesn't have good boundaries. He proclaims that "I shall delight in that. I'm just enjoying myself, and I'll take it the next time too." Daniel says he's not scary; he just doesn't know what he is doing. Perhaps this explains why, when Daniel and I would go out for lunch, the Fat Man would join us and somehow squeeze into a booth, which would make Daniel giggle hysterically. The Fat Man would say gibberish and other silly things that made no sense, like "Rubber baby buggy bumpers is a

Figure 12.3 *The Fat Man.*

baby buggy wooger" or "Why so many chi-ching (like a cash register) ding-dong yoyo."

The Sheriff says that the Fat Man understands nothing, but only the Sheriff can calm the Fat Man down when he acts up or has a temper tantrum. The Sheriff is an average-sized Native American man who wears big boots and black pants and has long black hair. He likes to yell loudly that he is THE SHERIFF! He lives on a ranch in South Carolina that he built himself. Daniel sees the ranch in his mind's eye. The Sheriff tries to keep order among the voices and tells people to act properly. He cracks the whip at the voices when necessary. He tells them, "To leave Dan alone." In the past, he threatened Daniel, but their relationship changed, and they became friends. "I came out

Figure 12.4 *The Sheriff.*

of a freezer to be Dan's gentle friend," he has said. He's not the leader, but he enforces the rules and protects people, including Daniel.

TJ was a voice that disappeared quickly. He was a punk, had a mohawk and spiked hair, and wore a leather jacket. He carried a club-like baseball bat in a backpack. When he hunched over, he could take the bat, swing it over his head, and pound someone. He hit Daniel three times until the Fat Man picked him up and threw him far away, never to be seen again.

When Daniel first met the Pimp, he was eating a cheese sandwich that the Pimp tried to take, and they had an argument. But they are now friends. The Pimp is a Black man who wears only white, weighs about 900 pounds, is present intermittently, but rides around in a white chauffeur-driven limo and will "shit out the window" without warning. Despite this, the Pimp is a good voice, and Daniel still sees him driving around. His speech is raspy and sounds like he has been smoking cigars for twenty years, reminding Daniel of Isaac Hayes's "Chef" character in the *South Park* television series.

The Community of Spirits was a raucous yet benign community until William showed up. Daniel was afraid of him from the beginning. William was seven feet tall, dressed like he worked in an office, wore elegant shoes, a suit, and a fancy watch. If things didn't go his way, he yelled and screamed obscenities, made a mess of everything, and threw papers around. He would scream at Daniel saying, "You're a faggot and there are ants in your fanny." He would yelp like a dog and defecate anywhere. When William was especially upset, he would kick over tables. Sometimes he pulled down his pants and exposed himself. He seemed totally "out of it" and would bark loudly. Once, he took the top off a water bubbler and peed in it. He touched Daniel inappropriately and was sexually provocative.

While Daniel was at Eikos, William was responsible for Daniel being transported deeper into his new reality. He experienced his physical body as intermittently chained to a table and his brain as independently "self-aware" and separated from his body. Green marbles kept emerging from his mouth. As William walked around the table, laughing at Daniel's plight, his body was overtaken by the Hell Maggots and Purgatory Leeches.

Unfriendly monks had suddenly arrived and encouraged the first appearance of the Hell Maggots, but all the voices talked about them. Because of his interest and study of insects and creatures, Daniel knows a great deal about how maggots operate in the "real" world, but the maggots associated with his community of spirits eat both live and dead animals and people. Although they may sound ghastly, Hell Maggots weren't "a problem because they aren't as bad as you think they might be even if they are very large." Drinking ginger ale or alcohol gets rid of them, so Daniel felt somewhat protected. The Sheriff said the maggots were created in New York by homeless people. "If they tortured mice in front of a dead animal that had maggots on it, the maggots mutated and burrowed into people, growing larger yet ultimately helping the person stay healthy. They can also come out of the ground and eat your shoes."

At Eikos the maggots burrowed through Daniel's cerebral cortex. After they had eaten enough, some of them became less intimidating. His voices told him

Figure 12.5 *Leroy, William, and Ed.*

the Hell Maggots would work for him and eat the sneakers off any unfriendly monks, which provided him with some protection. After their initial attack, they just hung around and stayed quiet, and they had their benefits because eating the dead flesh ultimately made Daniel healthier. After closing their burrow holes, they had done their work. According to Daniel, "If you are dead, the Hell Maggots send Purgatory Leeches to consume you."

The same unfriendly monks could beckon Purgatory Leeches to kill people. They can call these leeches from different parts of the world to devour people's bodies. Daniel described a babysitter who didn't get the job he wanted being eaten by the leeches. After he died, a man with long eyebrows and white hair picked up his skeleton and threw him into a sewer.

After the appearance of William, the voices became more threatening and malicious. From the beginning of Daniel's time at Eikos, William encouraged Daniel to act inappropriately. He showed him pictures of Daniel looking like a caveman in the *Flintstones* smashing things. Daniel's internal climate transformed. With the notable exception of Diesel, the voices—Fat Man, Sheriff, TJ, the Pimp, and especially William—became scary, punitive, and malevolent. They were joined by several others, particularly Ed and LeRoy—whom Daniel could barely tolerate. Years later, when he was volunteering at a community center and washing dishes, these three threatened to sodomize him if he washed one more spoon.

Ed is only a head, has dark hair, is partly Native American, has a giant face like a football, and is about thirty-five years old. He will try to kiss Daniel anywhere and is very annoying. Ed says he has to put his lips on people all day because "I have to give love, or I don't feel very well." He is the "biggest pain of all the voices." Daniel tried to ignore him by chewing gum or bouncing a tennis ball. Of all the voices, he is the worst, and Daniel had difficulty functioning when Ed appeared. He rarely talked to Daniel, but he would try to touch him. If Daniel ignored him, Ed would scream.

Another threatening voice that appeared around the same time was Leroy, who acted "retarded," had large elephant ears, was only five feet tall, was mixed race, and shaped like a refrigerator. Like Ed, he wanted to kiss Daniel and would say in a weird tone "I like kissing you." He harassed Daniel, but then Ed took over, insisting "If you don't let me put my lips on you, I will get violent and I will become violent and do it more." Only Ed and LeRoy tried to perform sexual acts on Daniel, but they were unrelenting, and it took years for Daniel to develop techniques to stop them.

Daniel lived in terror of William, Ed, and Leroy whose behavior escalated when Daniel was hospitalized at the Arbour a substandard mental hospital, but because he had no way to reality test their demands or their conversation, for a long time he remained secretive about the details of his experience except to say that the voices were torturing him, and they were unremitting. He couldn't function in their presence. According to Daniel they "drove me insane."

Over the years more voices appeared—about eleven in total. Many come and go, but some have stayed and are Daniel's dear friends. One of the most

Figure 12.6 *The Bishop.*

important is Bishop. She showed up around four years after Eikos. She is about eight feet tall, looks a lot like Lady Gaga, is pretty, and is a "great voice to have." She wears big boots, tight leggings, a long jacket, and a winter hat that is tall, pointy, with a pom-pom on the top, evoking a bishop on a chessboard. She tends to be quiet, is fun-loving, and dances, spinning around like at a disco ball. Her feet never touch the ground—she floats and hovers, even when she is ice skating. She likes to do different enjoyable things and has many interests. She likes Daniel to talk about her *a lot* and gets upset if he doesn't.

One of Bishop's most interesting qualities is that she has a little castle located inside her along with a monastery. Ten floating monks in brown robes live in the monastery. They are just there—neither helpful nor unhelpful. They meditate most of the time and occasionally talk to Daniel, telling him they flew across the ocean to visit him, saying, "'Oh, we are monks. Oh, we meditate. We Zen, we Zen!' They say things like that." Bishop may have captured the monks because they were giving away her thoughts and she was offended, but the monks don't mind because they now have a home.

Bishop doesn't say much to Daniel, but she is still there a lot of the time. As with Diesel, Daniel considers Bishop a close friend, one of his favorite voices, and misses her if he doesn't see her regularly. Interestingly, Diesel and the Bishop have never talked to each other.

Rabies is like Diesel; they are both bald and have easygoing personalities. He is another cool voice who showed up early and hasn't disappeared. Daniel first saw him across the room drinking coffee. He is about twenty-five years old, white, bald, and wears a T-shirt with Mickey Mouse on it, sweatpants, and Timberland boots. He has tattoos of moons with little circles on his wrists. He is "very nice," never gave Daniel any trouble, and doesn't talk much. He is not Christian, but he reads Bible verses in public parks and at home. He will occasionally yell, "Look, I'm a very lonely guy!" I believe he represents Daniel's aloneness. Daniel says that "It's very good having voices like those."

Sumumum appears as a giant moon hovering over a village called Motorheadville that is like a junkyard or comes to Daniel as a disgruntled old man walking around with a cane. Daniel often sees him feeding pigeons. He is sometimes irritable but otherwise has been nice to Daniel. He doesn't talk much. Daniel still sees him about once a month.

The Drill Instructor is a cool guy from the US Army who is in his fifties and is seven feet tall. He looks mean. Everyone addresses him as "Sir." He makes silly comments like "I wish I had a tapeworm," which often makes Daniel giggle. He's funny and is like Sergeant Hartman from *Full Metal Jacket*. The Drill Instructor talks to Daniel only occasionally. Scientists sometimes let him try out new weapons that the military has designed. He talks a lot about war in the Congo and people getting their hands and feet chopped off. He is important because he teaches new recruits. He has a son who has a "mind problem." The son is angry at him because "He doesn't let him do everything he wants to do in life." Daniel has hallucinated the son yelling, screaming, and pulling out knives and saying that his father never takes no for an answer.

Figure 12.7 *The Drill Instructor and Barilla.*

The Drill Instructor talks to Barilla often and says, "I got the foul mouth around here." He spends a lot of time hanging out with her; she is "an opposite polarity to him; they have opposite personalities but are good friends even though they come from different walks of life." Barilla is "pure hippy." She is a pretty, muscular woman who is cute, has long brown hair, is about 5'8" and wears a tie-dyed shirt with no bra, tattered jeans that have flower patches on them, and cheap sandals. She is an environmentalist, extremely concerned about the climate and always talks about "not wasting water or food." She doesn't want nature debased. She gets upset if Daniel doesn't finish his food or walks across live grass. She is concerned about environmental issues and doesn't want the earth's resources to be used up. She doesn't talk to Daniel much but will say, "You are doing so well right now" when he doesn't walk on a lawn or conserves water. He still sees her every few days.

Ms. Krabappel is Daniel's favorite *Simpsons* character. She is in her thirties and teaches the class that Bart Simpson is in. She is more serious than the other voices and tells him, "Life doesn't work out the way you want it to." Sometimes Daniel feels that nothing is good—he has no job experience, he never went to college, and he is unemployed. His life hasn't worked out the way he wanted it to; perhaps Ms. Krabappel represents his disappointment.

There are other less frequent voices. Helga dresses in black, likes to eat in food courts like Taco Bell, and says, "Peace to my chiojo (throat) biotch (Bitch)" even when the Fat Man yells at her. Another Pimp—Daniel doesn't know his name and they've never spoken—is Black, ten feet tall, dresses in purple clothes and fancy dress shoes that you would wear "if you worked in a high-rise building," and sometimes sneaks up on the voices and tries to talk sense into them, especially those that are nameless. Another voice is Captain Rhodes from *Dawn of the Dead*—a military commander who facilitated a civilian-run operation to conduct experiments on zombified human beings and who bangs on the table and screams, "I'm running the monkey farm now and I want to know what the fuck you are doing with my time?" Several other voices are Goth, including one who is covered in paint because he plays paintball all the time and another who wears dark sunglasses and says things like "Peach to chocko biotch."

When the voices first appeared at Eikos, Daniel was frightened and bewildered. He didn't try to get any help with them because of his confusion and feeling that he was part of the experience and inside of it. They were his reality. From my perspective as his mother, it was completely disturbing and made little sense at times. My transcriptions and descriptions of our conversations about this experience don't fully capture the horror of what Daniel endured, but thankfully it has become easier as time has passed.

The strategies Daniel has developed to cope with the voices include joining a Hearing Voices Group, part of the worldwide Hearing Voices Network. In the UK alone there are 189 groups and, in the US, more than 110 located in most states. They claim that 3–10 percent of the population—even more than Oliver Sacks acknowledged—"hear voices, see visions, or have other unusual perceptions" (Hearing Voices Network, 2024). These groups are part of the international Hearing Voices Movement that was established in the early 1990s to challenge the dominance of disease models and normalize the voices by respecting diverse explanations and by viewing them as part of the natural human experience and not merely a symptom of mental illness. Peer support and self-help groups create safe spaces for the voice hearer to explore the personal meaning of the voices, make sense of them, and encourage empowerment, pride, and self-respect (Garety, 2001; Longden, 2017).

Daniel found the groups supportive and helpful in reducing the stigma associated with his community of spirits. Their purpose is "helping to create respectful and empowering spaces" and to reduce the feelings of shame and aloneness. There is no presumption of illness. Sharing his experiences with other people who also hear voices has helped Daniel feel "less crazy," better understood, and empowered. According to the research, he is not alone (Longden et al., 2018).

While I was a young adult, I went to a hearing voices group which was on a beautiful campus of a psychiatric facility. There were other adults of all ages, and we talked about the voices that we would often hear. They were friendly and compassionate.

At the voices group we talked about our voices. Some people were very sick, and some people were quite well. One person was a pedophile who had called the police on himself. Another person had voices for fifteen years, but they went away because of the medication he took which was Seroquel. I would wear Bombas socks, and all the people there wanted to have socks of that quality which I found quite humorous. I talked about my voices as well. I would say which ones at the time would torment me like Ed, William, and Leroy. I would also talk about the benevolent ones as well like Diesel, Bishop, and The Pimp. I would grab a coffee and just sit down and talk.

The talk was just mostly small talk. Talk about the little things in life. Things we talked about were not only voices but things like what socks we would wear, sports, etc. It was a short meeting that was held in a small, borrowed room on the campus. It was next to the cafeteria. The people were on the less troubled side. They seemed stable as far I would be concerned. I took an Uber to the meeting. I then took an Uber back. I was never late because the meeting meant a lot to me. Anything at the time that could possibly help meant a lot to me.

Daniel has also developed various unique and personal strategies to deal with the voices when they interfere with his activities. Through his talk therapies, he has learned to talk back to them to find out if their threats are genuine. Daniel discovered that most threats were empty. Chewing gum helped a great deal because he was doing something active that gave him a feeling of agency and reduced his helplessness when he encountered them. Similarly, he wears various leather studded bracelets and rubber bands on his wrists that he can snap. When LeRoy was trying to kiss him on his cheeks, he would wear face cream. Sometimes, when the voices were at their most active and menacing, he would put tinfoil in his baseball cap in an effort to prevent the voices from getting into his head. Anything that made him feel less vulnerable and more empowered helped him function in the face of their chaos.

When I went to Home Depot, Leroy, William, and Ed stopped bothering me and I stopped seeing as much and hearing as much. Maybe walking through the aisles and sorting out all the products reconstructed my brain a little bit in some way. All the work they had for me took my mind off all my problems and I was focusing on the task at hand. When I worked in the garden center, being around living things like plants and selling people plants for their gardens may have cultivated some kind of good energy for me in some way that healed me. I don't know. Maybe it took my mind off everything. Maybe it was because I was independent and working, the captain of my own ship.

As Daniel has progressed in recovery, the voices are less of a bother and have receded into the background. Even the vicious voices—Ed, William, and LeRoy—diminished in intensity when Daniel started working at Home Depot about ten years after leaving Eikos. Most of the kinesthetic aspects have ended and although Leroy and William still appear in the shadows, they no longer physically harass him. Daniel feels he has learned how to manage them.

The Fat Man and the Pimp appear more frequently than some of the others who come and go and only occasionally cause him trouble. Diesel and Bishop remain important to Daniel and still tell him to do things. For example, he recently gained weight with their encouragement. They tell him to eat extra portions of food or to buy pastries when he is drinking coffee, although they know he is on a diet. Daniel has developed strategies for coping with them if they tell him to do things that are not in his best interest. He lives more comfortably side by side with them and views them as a support. To Daniel, they are a plus in his life and he looks forward to seeing them. They provide both solace and friendship.

> *My relationship with my voices is that I ignore them as much as I can. I do this because I would rather make my own decisions. They used to interfere with my day but now that they don't interfere with my day. I do not like to get into the habit of listening to them because they are not real. I wish I could tell you that they are spirit guides, but this is simply not true. I have gotten very tired of hearing them all these years. They tell me nothing truly helpful, yet if they are not helpful it is still a mere trifle to hear the worst of what one of them might say or show me these days. Only the Bishop and Diesel are welcome to appear before me and say what they say, but it's not a big event.*

13

Florid Psychosis

In the early days, the voices generally did not communicate directly with Daniel but would have circular conversations with each other, so after a while Daniel stopped listening to them. As I've said, they generally remained friendly, at least until William appeared on January 1, 2004—New Year's morning. William encouraged Daniel to take a baseball bat and smash the windows of six cars that were parked outside of the main house at Eikos. William demonstrated how to do it, and Daniel eventually complied, which led to his arrest at gunpoint.

The police were called and, with guns drawn, surrounded my nineteen-year-old son. It was lucky he wasn't shot, but he readily acquiesced to their commands. However, he was charged with multiple felonies requiring a court appearance later that year. An astute police officer noticed that Daniel was uncommunicative and acting bizarrely, and after a short visit to a general hospital ER, he was transferred to Arbour, where there was an available bed. That is when I went to see Daniel on a locked ward, and he asked me whether I heard the loud heavy metal music that was blasting. I didn't hear anything, and that's when I realized my son had experienced a florid—acute and full-blown—psychotic break, most likely schizophrenia, and was totally disorganized. He was hallucinating and delusional and out of contact with reality. I was stunned.

In the following weeks, more voices emerged that were loud, threatening, and accusatory. Ed, LeRoy, and a few others joined William. They screamed and yelled at Daniel constantly, torturing him. He spent his time pacing around the ward, out of contact with other people, internally distressed, and having almost no grip on reality. I visited mostly every day but was unable to engage him in any meaningful conversations. I sat with him or paced with him; there seemed little else to do.

Arbour Hospital was a nightmare, and the setting was inhumane. The staff took away Daniel's shoelaces and any electronic equipment, so he had nothing to keep him occupied. He was alone in a room where he slept on a cot with a plastic-covered mattress. He felt neglected, ignored, and just locked up. According to Daniel, "They just forgot about me and let me rot." He described meeting with the doctor for *seven* minutes a week! According to Daniel, the nurses taunted him, telling him that he would never get out of there.

My initial interaction with the staff was congenial but rapidly deteriorated. Treatment consisted primarily of multiple antipsychotic medications administered in rapid succession. No time was given between meds to figure out if they were effective. The staff would give him an antipsychotic drug, and if he didn't improve within a few days (which he didn't), they would add another drug. This type of polypharmacy only made things worse. As his behavior continued to deteriorate, Daniel spent more time in a seclusion room unless the environment was chaotic and patients were on edge, then the hospital would lock down the entire ward, and patients were required to stay in their rooms with the lights off. None of these strategies helped Daniel.

During the disastrous and lengthy hospitalizations at the Arbour, he was intermittently transferred to other facilities or to his father's home when the staff thought he could even marginally function outside the hospital, especially since he had only minimally improved, if at all. Ultimately, Daniel was discharged to his father's care on Cape Cod. There, he was closely supervised by his father (who was also a psychiatrist) as well as for a short time, by a case management team in Cambridge, Massachusetts, some distance away. Daniel's psychotic symptoms were unremitting, and he remained delusional and frightened. He thought that people were against him and were trying to "steal his brain." The voices increased and continued to mock him and tell him that he was "going to hell," leading to him becoming aggressive, agitated, and restless.

Daniel's behavior worsened despite his father's support, and he was taken to Falmouth Hospital ER, given IV Haldol, and then readmitted to Arbour in Boston for another disastrous hospitalization. After a short stay characterized by yet more polypharmacy and seclusion, he was transferred to a small general hospital unit at Beth Israel Deaconess Hospital on the presumption that he might have temporal lobe epilepsy and that his psychosis was a result of that. Over time, this diagnosis has been repeatedly questioned.

While in the hospital, Daniel was agitated, restless, and provocative. During my visits, he seemed totally out of contact with reality. "You're a demon!" he repeatedly asked me to spell my name slowly every time I talked to him. It became impossible to have a conversation.

The staff had difficulty managing him. Daniel made several "sandwiches" filled with shaving cream and gave them to two of the older demented patients, claiming it was just a prank. Later he said he did it purposefully because the patients "bugged the hell out of" him. He put notes under patients' doors in the middle of the night saying, "Suck my balls," set fire to some Styrofoam cups in the smoking room while insisting, "Blood will flow." He painted "Fuck you!" on his forehead. He was given few privileges, although his behavior improved somewhat over the course of this two-week hospitalization. Compared to the Arbour, which was like a state hospital, the environment in a general hospital was far more comforting, safer, better staffed, and helped Daniel to calm down. Furthermore, Daniel was not put into seclusion.

Over many months, Daniel improved slightly after being additionally medicated with mood stabilizers and anti-seizure meds, but was still psychotic, delusional, internally preoccupied, and withdrawn. He was then sent to a residential program called Wild Acres in Lexington, Massachusetts, but they were totally unprepared for someone with his degree of difficulty. His short stay was characterized by noncompliance, belligerence, and frequent absences from the program without permission. After he pulled their fire alarms and disappeared, I spent several days with the help of a friend tracking him down and finally found him in Harvard Square hanging out with a group of unhoused men. The possibility of never finding my son was terrifying. I was frightened by how much he had deteriorated and how radically his psychotic symptoms had worsened.

I've been diagnosed schizophrenic for a very long time, ever since nineteen. And it was never dangerous in my opinion, but it was not controlled. And mental illness needs to be controlled and monitored. And I think it's very taxing on an entire family. When a family has somebody that falls to mental illness, it's a total disaster for everybody. Not just the person that has that mental illness because they have to spend all their money now on doctors and not have that guy go away to college and be successful. They have to deal with hospitalizations, they have to deal with meds, and they have to deal with living with a crazy person. And nobody wants to do that.

Everyone involved in Daniel's care was bewildered and perplexed about what to do next but agreed it was safest for him to return to his father's home on Cape Cod—a quiet rural area. We needed to figure out how we could help him. At his father's house, Daniel did not improve, and if anything, his symptoms worsened—he drifted further out of touch. His father described his psychotic behavior, saying Daniel paced constantly, was agitated, non-communicative, and restless. He screamed and yelled at the voices. He walked around with quarters in his ears and made an aluminum foil hat to reduce the transmission of thoughts into his brain from the voices that were torturing him. He performed rituals such as making circles of sea salt on the outside deck and sitting for hours inside the circle to remain "safe." Occasionally, he came to his father's bedroom at night, threatening him and laughing hysterically. Because of Daniel's deteriorating behavior, he was again admitted to the Arbour. This was his third admission there and fourth hospitalization in less than a year—and during this time, despite the medication, family support, and some case management, he became more deeply entrenched in a scary and threatening alternate world.

The hospitals were horrifying. The pits. Human garbage dumps. It's an oppressive, horrible environment where you have awful doctors that just leave you there. I felt forgotten about by the whole world. I spent most of my time pacing and sleeping. The doctors gave me a bad rap saying that I "should rot in a dark black cell" and I did not feel safe. Some of the nurses felt threatening if I didn't do what they said. I feel like they did not care and were just "doing their job." There was no greater relief for me than being discharged from the hospitals.

Nothing had helped Daniel, and in fact, his illness seemed to worsen despite good intentions, an army of experts, and what we thought at that time was a reasonable treatment plan. His illness was devastating and unremitting, so we decided to start again and removed him from the traditional hospital system, which had little to offer. We decided to see if we could change his course and interrupt what at the time appeared to be an inevitable decline. It turned out to be one of the best decisions we made.

With help from a colleague and friend, we were able to arrange for Daniel to be transferred to a small fourteen-bed catchment area hospital called High Point in Plymouth (near Cape Cod). They were willing to waive the residential rules and agreed to admit him.

When Daniel was admitted to High Point, the clinicians attending him noted he "was disheveled, unshaven, tired" and that he exhibited "thought blocking, thought insertion and withdrawal, delusions and hallucinations." Upon admission, he was taking a smorgasbord of medications: Lamictal, Keppra, Seroquel, Risperdal, Haldol, Cogentin, Benadryl, and Chlorothiazide. He had become a psychotic "zombie," and the addition of Benadryl only capped their wish to totally sedate him, which they did. He refused to discuss any issues, was preoccupied with auditory and visual hallucinations, revealed thoughts of hurting himself, and was aggressive.

The plan was to slowly wash out all the medications from his system and start again, this time with Clozaril. Until then, I had been opposed to giving him this, what was at the time the latest antipsychotic drug, because it was new, and it could cause bone marrow suppression and a sometimes fatal blood disorder called agranulocytosis. When we started Clozaril, Daniel finally began to have a glimmer of the other reality—and entertained the idea that the voices were not real. He begged to have their volume turned down, which the Clozaril helped with over time. It seemed like a slim beginning, but at least it represented a possibly hopeful restart. Getting him out of the traditional system was the best thing we did during this challenging period.

Table 13.1 Daniel's High Point Medical Chart

10/13/04	Slept poorly, oppositional, odd behaviors
10/20/04	Increased auditory hallucinations
10/21/04	Increase in disturbing voices, past several days/but appeared more appropriate to staff
10/25/04	Voices are worse, but also said they were "quieter, not as bothersome"
10/26/04	Voices increasing
11/4/04	Stated he was doing "pretty good," but when questioned further stated he was "not doing well" due to auditory hallucinations
11/13/04	Isolated and withdrawn; still hearing voices that are derogatory
11/19/04	Daniel was confused—said he was "doing well," then changed to "not doing well," became angry, walked away, still had auditory hallucinations
11/24/04	Daniel switched to a less restrictive unit, but almost immediately had an altercation with another patient and was sent back to the locked unit
12/1-2/04	Signed three-day paper. "He still hears voices" (case manager); discharged to family (father on the Cape)", no follow up care or plan, prognosis guarded

In my files, I found his medical chart, which describes his course in the hospital: The staff expected a length of stay of "two to three months" and felt that he would not be able to live independently at the end of that time. He left High Point after fifty days, and although the voices had become less strident, little else had changed. Daniel had spent almost a full year in hospitals—a year when most young men his age are finishing college and starting their adult lives—and was only slightly improved. We were worried about how distressed he felt and what this meant about the nature of his illness and potential for the future.

14

Our Broken Mental Health System

How Did We Get Here?

Daniel's move from High Point Hospital to an apartment on Cape Cod, and then a few years later to Side by Side (SBS), a residential program in Brookline, was a turning point that reflected the national shift of care from mental hospitals into the community. Although Daniel was still psychotic, with adequate support and time, he was able to adjust to life outside an institution. We were fortunate to have the resources to bypass the public system and the profound disparities between public and private treatment and care. We doubled down on our efforts to hire our own treatment team, one that included providers with lived experience—now called peer specialists, peer workers, or peer supporters[1]—a decision at the time based on our increasing disillusionment with the more traditional mental health system.

Overall, we felt that providers with lived experience were more empathic, more able to relate to Daniel as a person, and did not have as many implicit biases about serious mental illness. They maintained a hopeful attitude and were not afraid of Daniel's unique perceptions. Our beliefs dated back to

---

[1]It wasn't until 2021 that SAMHSA created an "Office of Recovery" and clearly stated that "recovery is enhanced by peer support services" and added that they were now critical workers with the severity of staffing shortages.

Daniel's adolescence when we hired two non-mental health providers to work with him during his homeschooling years. They saw Daniel as a person, not a label, and formed meaningful relationships with him. In fact, many years later he is still in contact with them.

Daniel's experience also raises the question of the role of the mental hospital in the Recovery process. He was hospitalized at least ten times before he was twenty-two, and during that time, his overall course was downhill. From my perspective, both as a mom and a psychiatrist, the major function of the mental hospital is to ensure the patient's safety and eventual stabilization. But have the hospitals accomplished this? They didn't with Daniel; his year in the hospital was a nightmare.

Volumes have been written about the different conceptions of "madness" and the history of how we have cared for the mentally ill among us. A very brief review of how we have treated the most seriously ill patients within the traditional mental health system is mirrored by some of our current challenges in providing care, including overcrowding, long wait lists, dangerous hospital conditions, staffing shortages, and stigma, and how care has ebbed and flowed between reforms and inadequate, even punitive treatment. From colonial times to the present, the pendulum keeps swinging with some reforms persisting. Some of the new directions are hopeful—especially the Recovery movement, increasing certification of peer specialists as well as the judicious use of medication and our increasing knowledge of the brain. However, our attention to the care of seriously mentally ill patients remains limited, and stigma and implicit biases persist (Grinker, 2021).

The story of mental health care in America began in colonial times when population density was so low there was little need for institutions (Hamm et al., 2020). Those who were "distracted" or considered "mad" were the responsibility of local communities and families. Mental illness was misunderstood, and patients were seen as dangerous and unfit. The Poor Laws, essentially an early labeling method, categorized the "underserving" or "impotent" poor, including those with mental illness who were placed in almshouses, workhouses, and jails after mandated removal from the community. Those in charge were fearful and often resorted to abusive treatment. Family caregivers were also ill-equipped to deal with their sick relatives, which often led to inhumane treatment provided out of ignorance (Yanni, 2007).

The introduction of specialized care in the mid-eighteenth century marked a welcome change in direction. Physician Benjamin Rush, the "father of American psychiatry," was the first to state his belief that mental illness is a disease of the mind and not a "possession of demons." *Observations and Inquiries upon the Diseases of the Mind*, published in 1812, was the first psychiatric textbook printed in the United States" (Penn Medicine, 2017). Rush was the first to suggest that mentally ill individuals should be treated in hospital settings (Carlson & Simpson, 1964). By 1844, there were twenty-five public and private mental hospitals in the entire country where care initially remained inhumane (Eghigian, 2009). The Quakers and then nineteenth-century French physician Philippe Pinel promoted "moral treatment," in which inadequate conditions and harsh punishment gave way to compassionate caretaking ultimately aimed at returning patients to the community. Pinel observed that "to detain maniacs in constant seclusion and to load them with chains; to leave them defenseless, [*sic*] to the brutality of underlings . . . is a system of superintendence, more distinguished for its convenience than for its humanity or its success" (Pinel, 1983). Concepts of medical illness supplanted those of social deviance as medical treatment became the primary reason for hospitalization. Under Pinel's guidance, a new standard for the care of individuals with mental illness replaced poorhouses and prisons and was reinforced by improved recovery rates (Grob, 1994). However, implementation of Pinel's vision was met with obstacles.

By the mid-nineteenth century, in the spirit of Pinel-inspired American activist Dorothea Dix, a crusade began to establish public mental health institutions that provided humane medical treatment to everyone who needed it. Dix was by far one of the most effective advocates and traveled across the US, gathering information about the "distresses of the insane" and presenting her findings to state legislatures and the US Congress (Ovsiew & Munich, 2008). She advocated for public policies that ensured "moral treatment" in the hospitals. In her petition to Congress in 1848, she described case after case of people declared "insane" who were kept in "utter neglect and squalid wretchedness" in poorhouses, almshouses, jails, shacks, and other settings, such as "pens, stalls, cages, and dungeons." Each story she related was more horrifying than the next:

> In one poorhouse was a man who had been chained by the leg for more than twenty years, and the only warmth introduced into his cell was derived from a small stovepipe carried through one corner. . . . the cells in the cellar for the insane were in a most wretched condition... The insane were miserably housed, fed, and clothed. In the vicinity of the main building was one of brick, containing the poor cells. From eight to nine feet square. A straw bed and blanket on the floor constituted the furniture, if I except the ring bolts and iron chains for securing the patients . . . I found the insane poorly provided for. One madman was chained, clothed only with a straight jacket, laced so as to impede the motion of the arms and hands; cold, exposed, and offensive to the last degree, his aspect wild and furious. (Dix, 1971)

Consequently, the hospital system gradually introduced reforms centered on moral treatment. But as the country grew, patients with diverse and often incurable needs such as syphilis, dementia, and aging who had no place to go or nobody to care for them were dumped into these institutions. As people with complex needs were transferred from homes and jails, hospitals became overcrowded and overwhelmed. Fewer patients were discharged. Initially, scale and cost were not considered, but as the hospitals grew and the numbers of patients increased, the difficulties of providing humane care also increased. While moral treatment in smaller facilities prevailed for more than a century, Dix's vision was never fully realized. As the patient population became more diverse and the proportion of chronically ill patients increased, the hospitals became overcrowded, care deteriorated, and people lost faith in the possibility of recovery and return to the community. These developments were reinforced by German physician Emil Kraepelin's formulation of dementia praecox in 1893 as an incurable progressive illness requiring institutionalization. (Jablensky, 2010). Eugen Bleuler coined the word "schizophrenia" in 1908 (Wang, 2019). Coupled with the emergence of eugenics, in which it was believed that desirable heritable traits could be manipulated, dangerous somatic interventions followed. This included psychosurgery and sterilization of patients who were viewed as incurable and unfit (Ebert & Bär, 2010).

By early in the twentieth century, the network of state hospitals, once a proud tribute to the era of reform, had largely turned into a bureaucratic morass within which patients were confined, often neglected, and sometimes abused (Bassuk & Gerson, 1978). Discharge rates fell precipitously. Hospitals were underfunded, understaffed, and overcrowded, creating punitive and coercive environments. Additionally, many believed that patients with behavioral disorders were among the most "unfit" and should be essentially incarcerated in hospitals, away from society.

During the early period of moral treatment, more than half of the patients had been discharged; however, by the first half of the twentieth century, many spent decades and sometimes their entire lives in state mental hospitals. One of the grimmest aspects of these policies was reflected in the recent emergence of many cemetery restoration projects, spearheaded by disability rights activist Patricia Deegan. She described how it gave families and ex-patients a chance to grieve, organize, and deal with the press (Penney & Stastny, 2008). It was also during this period that an array of somatic therapies was increasingly used, including lobotomies, as well as insulin and electroconvulsive therapies. The period ranging from 1900 to 1950 was one of the darkest in the history of mental health care in America. This was in stark contrast to the myriad scientific and medical achievements during this period, including those by Einstein, Hubble, and Salk.

Spurred by the unacceptable conditions of the state hospitals, calls for reform and the movement toward deinstitutionalization emerged. In 1946, the National Mental Health Act was passed, which provided funding for psychiatric research and education. This was followed by the establishment of the National Institute of Mental Health (NIMH) (Baker & Benjamin, 2005). Mental health advocates were not only angered by the deplorable conditions of hospitalized patients but also took issue with the institutional model. Among these advocates were twentieth-century Italian psychiatrist and neurologist Franco Basaglia, who rejected the use of seclusion and restraint and promoted the liberty and autonomy of patients (Foot, 2015), and sociologist Erving

Goffman (2007) who cautioned against the inherent stigma and biases created by institutional care.

Beginning in the 1950s with the introduction of chlorpromazine (Thorazine) and then other antipsychotic medications, state hospitals began releasing patients and community mental health services began to proliferate (Ban, 2007). The possibility arose that thousands of patients considered manageable only within the confines of the hospital could now be treated as outpatients. These changes led the way to President Kennedy's "bold new approach" with the passage in 1963 of the Mental Retardation Facilities and Community Mental Health Centers Construction Act, marking "a new approach to mental illness and to mental retardation. The Act is designed in large measure to use federal resources to stimulate state, local, and private action. When carried out, reliance on the cold mercy of custodial isolation will be supplanted by the open warmth of community concern and capability. Emphasis on prevention, treatment, and rehabilitation will be substituted for a desultory interest in confining patients in institutions to wither away" ("Community Mental Health Act," 2024).

Kennedy's concept of community mental health implied a dual promise of treatment and rehabilitation of the seriously mentally ill within the community and the general promotion of mental health (Bassuk & Gerson, 1978). Supported by the creation of Medicare and Medicaid in 1965, the transition to community-based care seemed like an attainable outcome (Foot, 2015). Within eight years, almost 400 community centers were operational (Hamm et al., 2020). However, the shortcomings of the initial legislation, the lack of adequate follow-up, insufficient funding, community resistance, and the uncertainties of effective therapies led to disappointing results. Over the next decades, the pendulum has swung again. The existing community-based system of support remains inadequate to meet the demand. Mental health services did not grow rapidly enough to keep pace with the growth in population. The result was homelessness, mass incarceration, and inhumane treatment in many of the remaining mental hospitals. I experienced this firsthand when I worked as a psychiatry resident at Boston State Hospital in the 1970s and in the decades that followed, as my career path propelled me toward advocacy for people experiencing homelessness.

The major impetus for deinstitutionalization was the belief that most psychiatric patients could be safely treated in community facilities if such facilities were available. The idea was basically sound, but its implementation was flawed and, sadly, Kennedy's dream was never realized. State hospital beds continued to play a critical role for a subset of individuals. According to the Treatment Advocacy Center (TAC), these included the following patients:

- uninsured and indigent
- criminal defendants deemed "unrestorable" who remain in the hospital under civil commitment
- defendants being evaluated for criminal responsibility who are using the insanity defense
- individuals who are violent or dangerous to themselves or others.
- jail inmates who need evaluation or treatment stand trial.
- pretrial defendants needing treatment to become competent to stand trial
- various individuals involved with the criminal justice system, including
- convicted prisoners who need intensive psychiatric care (Fuller et al., 2016).

Strategies for humanely managing the estimated 25 percent of psychiatric patients who do not respond to treatment and therefore cannot survive in a community setting without extensive supports and care have been unaddressed leaving individuals with serious mental illness at considerable risk.

The Treatment Advocacy Center in Arlington, Virginia, a nonprofit organization dedicated to eliminating barriers to the timely and effective treatment of serious mental illness, conducted a survey in 2016 about the number of state psychiatric hospital beds remaining after the peak of deinstitutionalization and found that "those beds are going, going, gone." They documented a "96.5% decrease from peak hospital numbers of approximately 560,000 public hospital beds in the 1950s to a new low of 37,679 beds (11.7 beds per 100,000 people) left in the 50 US states and D.C. This means that there are fewer state hospital beds per capita than at any time since before the nation stopped criminalizing mental illness in the 1850s" (Fuller et al., 2016). Forensic patients occupied almost half of these remaining beds. Bed shortages are a hardship for the patients who need them, and there is competition between forensic patients and civil patients. Policy analysts estimate that 40–60 inpatient beds per 100,000 people are required to meet the need.

Not only has the shrinking shortage of hospital beds contributed to the deplorable state of America's mental health care, but there is also a relative lack of private beds and long-term community residential options. Additional factors contributing to these circumstances include the indisputable relationship between mental health issues and poverty, discriminatory Medicaid and Medicare reimbursement practices, state mental health budget cuts, and difficulties accessing mental health professionals. Many believe that mental hospitals, when properly staffed and run, are the ultimate safety net for people with serious mental illness (Fuller, 1988).

Even further compounding this situation is the relative lack of essential mental health workers and severe staffing shortages primarily related to distribution across regions. For example, many more psychiatrists practice in urban locations, and within those urban areas in high-income neighborhoods. Furthermore, many do not accept Medicaid and commercial insurance (Insel, 2022, p. 99). According to Treatment Advocacy Center (TAC) studies from 2016, 55 percent of the nation's 3,100 counties have no practicing psychiatrists, psychologists, or social workers, and 40 percent of the nation's psychiatrists are older than fifty-five years and heading toward retirement. Furthermore, another recent report documented that between 1996 and 2016, the number of psychiatrists practicing psychotherapy significantly declined. In the 2010s, "about half of psychiatrists practiced no psychotherapy at all, creating new challenges to the integration of neurobiological and psychosocial elements of clinical care" (Tadmon & Olfson, 2022). In a December 2023 report by HRSA describing the Behavioral Health Workforce, substantial shortages are projected to continue in the future through at least 2036 (the end of their study). Currently, more than half of Americans live in a "mental health professional shortage area," and rural areas are most affected. A recent Massachusetts study (Bartlett, 2022) documented the beginning of a reversal of this trend with a small increase in beds, but the facilities are too short-staffed to admit patients to fill those beds. Combined with the lack of affordable housing and essential residential community programs, the situation for people with serious mental health problems remains almost as challenging as it was a century ago.

In 2012, TAC published a report describing some of the consequences of closing public psychiatric hospitals, a trend that has continued. They described shorter stays in poorly staffed hospitals, pressure on emergency rooms to care for the larger numbers of psychiatric patients, increased demands on law enforcement who became frontline mental health workers, and most of all the dramatic increase in patients incarcerated in prisons and jails, and the tragic growth of people living on the streets (Treatment Advocacy Center, 2012).

Understandably, by the 1980s, the prison population was growing, and with it, the proportion of prisoners with serious mental health issues (Nellis, 2024). Unprepared and untrained to deal with these individuals, the conditions in the prisons were often worse than in the asylums. According to the Vera Institute of Justice, although the "United States is home to less than 5 percent of the world's population, nearly 16 percent of all incarcerated people—roughly two million people—are held in our jails and prisons. We incarcerate more people per capita than any country in the world" (World Prison Brief, n.d.). Based on another recent report by TAC, ten times more individuals with serious mental illness are in jails and state prisons rather than in the remaining state hospitals (Torrey et al., 2014). They have become the "new asylums"; overcrowding, victimization, and use of solitary confinement often exacerbated mental health issues (Alexander, 2020).

According to the Bureau of Justice statistics, more than 80,000 people are still in solitary confinement in American prisons (Solitary Watch, 2025). "Too many prisoners, including the seriously mentally ill and juveniles, are locked away for 23 hours a day, often with little to no due process and at steep costs to the taxpayer," according to Senior Advisor to the Biden administration Cedric L. Richmond (Alpert, 2015).

Stories of solitary confinement both in mental hospitals and prisons abound. One of the most compelling, *Solitary*, was written by Albert Woodfox and was a finalist for the Pulitzer Prize. It tells of his forty years in solitary confinement in the infamous Angola Prison in Louisiana—a deprived, lonely existence in a six by nine-foot cell twenty-three hours a day (Woodfox, 2019). He was isolated for a crime he did not commit. The book poignantly describes how he turned his bitter and angry feelings into productive resistance and activism, a remarkable feat of personal strength (Woodfox, 2019). Unfortunately, this is not an isolated story since solitary confinement, seclusion, and restraint are common ways of managing both prisoners and patients. Overall, trans-institutionalization to our prison system has been a major fallout of the failures in the implementation of deinstitutionalization. The prisons have become the new asylums.

Along with the increasing prison population, the growth in homelessness also reflects some of the failures in creating a wrap-around community mental health system. Many people with serious mental illness and substance use disorders live on the streets and in shelters.

In 2023, HUD's Annual Homelessness Assessment Report to Congress documented that on a single night in January, 653,100 people were unhoused, representing approximately twenty of every 10,000 people, with homelessness increasing (U.S. Department of Housing and Urban Development, 2023). But this number has continued to rise. According to the New York *Times* on December 27, 2024, "The number of people experiencing homelessness topped 770,000, an increase of 18 percent over last year and the largest annual jump since the count began in 2007" (DeParle, 2024). Based on a report from HUD, the article goes on to state, "Nearly every category of unhoused people grew, with the rise especially steep among children (33 percent) and people in families (39 percent). The number of people in shelters rose by about a quarter, while unsheltered homeless rose 7 percent. The rise in homelessness among older adults continued as well, with a 6 percent growth in those 65 or older" (DeParle, 2024). Many of these people were unsheltered, doubled up, or staying in abandoned buildings and other places not suitable for human habitation. As in previous years, African Americans and Indigenous people were overrepresented. A significant percentage of these people suffer from chronic mental illness, most often with co-occurring disorders. According to TAC, one-third of the chronically homeless people with serious mental illness, and a greater number have substance use disorders.

History has taught us that neither the hospital nor the community are inherently more humane, but rather that social justice issues and civil rights must be combined with moral treatment and recovery approaches. Over the past half century, progress has been made to reduce the abuses that have plagued the system, particularly the use of seclusion and restraint and other dehumanizing and coercive practices. However, hospitals have a long way to go and still have not figured out how to adequately care for the subset of seriously mentally ill patients. This was certainly Daniel's experience during his hospitalization at the Arbour.

> *I didn't feel safe. There were very scary people, and I had no freedom. The only freedom was going to the smoke room and having a cigarette, which led to me smoking more. There was nothing to do on the unit, and I was generally left alone to wander around in the dayroom. If I became agitated, they would throw me into seclusion, put leather buckles on my hands and feet, and inject me with Haldol. They would threaten me by saying, "You will never get out if you don't shave in the morning." They would threaten to bring in security guards who would force me. I had no one to talk to. The environment was oppressive, gloomy, and dreary. I had a very melancholy feeling all the time and could hardly believe I was there.*

Since then, trauma-informed care has recently emerged as an organizing principle within the Recovery movement, and further progress has been made. These gains have been reinforced by the work of the President's Freedom Commission on Mental Health and the Substance Abuse and Mental Health Services Administration (SAMHSA), founded in 2002, yet despite the progress that has been made and the leadership of many mental health authorities, services for these individuals remain underfunded. Furthermore, the emergence of managed care has complicated the picture. "The changing financial and political landscapes, in combination with increased treatment of persons with serious mental illness (SMI) in prisons rather than the community, led to a cultural shift regarding the meaning of wellness in relation to SMI" (Hamm et al., 2020).

The New Freedom Commission Report provided recommendations for the vision of mental health in the twenty-first century: Recovery-oriented care should be the guiding framework. Even in 2003, they embraced the principles of the Recovery movement, and it was catalyzed by hope, purpose, and self-determination. Recovery was not equated with curing a disease but rather supporting persons with serious mental illness to live lives of purpose and meaning and to participate fully in the broader community. The challenge now is to bring Recovery practices to scale in hospitals and in the community through adequate legislation and funding and to address the pervasiveness of stigma, discrimination, and implicit bias about serious mental illness that underlies health care and is still rampant in our systems and society.

To date, community programs have more fully embraced and implemented Recovery-based programs than inpatient settings. Reviews of studies of psychiatric hospitals have highlighted an array of problems in which the biomedical model still predominates, and there are strong issues of oppression, power, and control, as well as the continuing widespread use of seclusion and restraint, limited access to supportive services such as psychotherapies, the ward milieu, inattention to trauma, and racial/ethnic disparities in care. Staff shortages compound these problems. Daniel's hospital experience reflects these serious issues (Carr, 2024). How will they be adequately addressed to reform the system . . . or will they?

15

Transforming Psychiatry

Since colonial times, the pendulum of American mental health care has swung back and forth between the community and hospitals. We have learned that neither the hospital nor the community approach is inherently more humane or effective (Bassuk & Gerson, 1978). The problem goes well beyond location. The DSM describes symptoms and diagnoses but does not relate them to treatment. Various psychotherapies have been developed that go beyond psychoanalytic treatment and focus on specific behavioral or cognitive targets, where skill learning is the basis for change but according to Insel, "are not widely available or adjusted to individual patient needs and often only focus on short-term issues" (Insel, 2022, p. 51).

There are few evidence-based protocols that include an explication of underlying brain mechanisms. And for serious mental illnesses, there are even fewer approaches to treatment, with the exception of the judicious use of selected medications. In addition to these limitations, the overall health care system has transformed into big business motivated by the bottom line and reflected in staffing shortages, limited bed capacity, and a wide gap between need and access. This has had unacceptable implications for the many people with serious mental illness and raises questions about the role of psychiatry within the glaring deficiencies in our health care system.

As the journalist Pete Earley described in *Crazy: A Father's Search Through America's Mental Health Madness*, psychiatrists prescribed his son, who was suffering from serious mental illness, a "dizzying range of drugs and different therapies," most of which did not help (Earley, 2007; Insel, 2022). This too was our experience, and it led, over the many decades of Daniel's illness, to my disillusionment with psychiatry and distrust of the health care system. Most of all, it raised many questions, including: Daniel's symptoms and diagnoses, his relationship to his healthcare providers, the role of stigma, the impact of trauma, treatment options, the role of environmental stressors, and the place of psychiatry as a humanistic specialty. These questions, coupled the transformation of the health care system into big business, show that mental health care needs a complete overhaul.

The health care system and psychiatry have changed dramatically since I was a young medical student and psychiatry resident in the 1970s. My journey through the mental health world has paralleled many of the changes in the system. My involvement formally began in the early 1970s when I became a resident in psychiatry because it was the most person-centered specialty. I believed deeply in its compassionate model of care and its accompanying psychodynamic framework and talk therapies. My residency program at Beth Israel Hospital in Boston was based on an authentic appreciation for individual needs and a respect for the uniqueness of our patients. However, in those mid-twentieth-century years, there were disturbing exceptions to this view; we still did not know how best to treat individuals with serious mental illnesses, nor did we understand much of the neuroscience or genetics underlying them.

Anthropologist Gregory Bateson popularized the label of the "schizophrenogenic mother" (Bateson et al., 1956; Hartwell, 1996) which was "a negative stereotype found in the psychiatric literature of the 1950s through to the 1970s. It refers to mothers of individuals who develop schizophrenia, the implication being that the mother has induced the illness . . ." (Seeman, 2016). I too initially believed that mothers were to blame for their child's affliction. I guiltily recall an eighteen-year-old patient who was hallucinating and paranoid, whose mother was struggling. With the support of my supervisor, I refused to deal with her mother and blamed her for her daughter's serious illness. I wish I could undo how I treated her because I became that mother.

Throughout the years, I encountered many caretakers and professionals who outright blamed me—often leading to shame, doubt, and wavering confidence about the path we were taking and my ability to adequately mother him. Even on Daniel's worst days, I never thought he was hopeless. I was anxious and fearful about what his illness portended, what it meant for his care and what to do, but I always had faith that there had to be a way to help him. So, I began to look toward Recovery-oriented systems of care and its four supportive dimensions: health, home, purpose, and community (Substance Abuse and Mental Health Services Administration, n.d.). The Recovery movement which slowly emerged from the addiction world in the late twentieth century (International Mental Health Collaborating Network, n.d.), reshaped many of my views about patients with mental illness and helped catapult me on a path of hope for Daniel's future.

An early turning point in my career was my decision not to become a psychoanalyst—a subspecialty that tended to attract the brightest and most creative among my colleagues. In my view, it was an elite subspecialty that saw a few patients intensively and was unavailable and not especially relevant to people living near or in poverty or those with serious mental illness. Psychoanalysis in those days generally attracted patients who comprised the so-called "worried well," who were able to afford many therapy sessions weekly. However, people such as Daniel were not candidates for this type of treatment. Few psychoanalysts or talk therapists treated patients with diagnoses like psychosis. There were certainly notable exceptions; Elyn Saks describes in her riveting memoir *The Center Cannot Hold* how her intensive lifelong therapy was, in part, responsible for helping her manage her psychotic illness and function at a high level (Saks, 2008). Until recently, I had tremendous difficulty finding a psychiatrist who agreed to ongoing "talk therapy" with Daniel because he was labeled schizophrenic. However, with a superb referral, in 2023 we found Dr. Michael Garrett, who has engaged him in an authentic relationship, has helped him understand and manage his voices, and has helped to "normalize" his experience. In many ways, he is the exception that proves the rule. Daniel now talks about his "imagination brimming over" and understands that the voices represent the part of himself expressing his desires and wishes.

Paradoxically, many psychiatrists (including myself) were also patients in analysis. It was part of the general ethic transmitted by my supervisors when I was a resident. Understanding yourself and working through your issues made you a better therapist. Probably true. However, I wondered over the years with my brilliant therapist Dr. John Mack what I had gained personally except a trusting, supportive relationship that helped with the many stresses in my complicated life. He unwaveringly supported me in my male-dominated workplace and with the pressures at home—my marriage and children. Because of his unconventional and daring views—particularly his interest in alternative therapies—he was a magnificent, albeit controversial, role model who supported the unique road I eventually took as a psychiatrist and influenced some of my later nontraditional professional choices.

Instead of becoming an analyst, I initially conducted psychodynamic psychotherapy and developed a thriving clinical practice with many patients over a period of twenty-five years. Over those decades, I tried to learn and integrate specific behavioral and cognitive approaches that were more skills-based. I saw the so-called "worried well," but also, unlike many of my peers, treated patients with serious mental illness—all requiring compassionate care, respect, understanding, and some needing medication. Most of my patients came in weekly for fifty-minute sessions, and if they were in a crisis, I made myself available by phone or for additional appointments. However, many patients had the added burden of dealing with the impact of poverty, such as lack of affordable housing and racism.

Through my experiences as a therapist and a psychiatric resident, I began to understand that there was a real split in the work that I did. Severe psychotic illnesses such as schizophrenia and bipolar disorder were viewed as catastrophic and often hopeless. I learned this as a resident when I ran the ward at Boston State Hospital for extremely disturbed patients, applying my experience to the challenges of caring for this generally unwanted subgroup. Not only were they unwanted, but the tools of the trade, with the exception of medication, were sparse, and best practices leading to positive outcomes were minimal. We simply didn't know how to treat these patients except to chemically restrain them with sedating medications. Sadly, many had neither supports, insurance, nor a place to go.

Although the old Kraepelinian view of dementia praecox as a devastating, deteriorating illness was predominant in those earlier years, as time went on and Recovery strategies began to dominate, this picture has been modified and imbued with hope. We have learned that even people with the most serious mental illnesses can learn to manage their symptoms, live independently in the community, and fulfill some of their dreams. Furthermore, approximately 25 percent or more fully recover from the first episode (National Institute of Mental Health, 2022). And many others can live lives with purpose, hope, and fulfilling relationships while managing their symptoms. They are human, as are we all.

In my first job outside of residency, when I oversaw the psychiatric emergency room (ER) at Beth Israel Hospital, most of my patients were in crisis, extremely ill, and had no place to turn. The ER was chaotic, scary, and crowded. I had to deal with the overflow from the diminishing number of beds in public mental hospitals, the shrinking of the workforce, and the increasing numbers of people who were discharged to jails and the streets. On wintry, snowy days, I was reluctant to put people out into the cold, many without a home, and instead kept them in the ER. I sent them to the cafeteria or "pink papered" them to a public mental hospital down the street where we had a revolving door; the public hospital would usually return them after seventy-two hours because they had no place to go. I was severely admonished for keeping these patients in the hospital. When I discharged a patient without indicating a placement, I had to consult our hospital attorney to affirm this unacceptable practice, but there were few options.

As a psychiatrist trained in the 1970s and 80s, I deeply believed in the values of that period, but was caught in a system that didn't know how to compassionately treat the sickest and poorest among us. Crisis care in the ER reflected psychiatry's lack of knowledge, although many of us still maintained the ability for empathic interactions. When I think back to how I occasionally dealt with patients using four-point restraints and IM Haldol, I can only cringe, particularly when I now talk to patients, including my son, who recount the trauma of being rendered helpless and the terror associated with these experiences. I learned about this firsthand when Daniel was in the sixth grade at Manville and was four-point restrained for his Tourette tics, and again later when he was hospitalized and repeatedly restrained. I railed against these interventions. Who could have foreseen that my professional conflicts were also going to play out in my personal life?

I remember feeling fearful when a patient was out of control in the ER—a relatively small space with many severely ill patients. There seemed to be no other way to manage them, but who was I in this situation as a caretaker and a young doctor? I can rationalize these interventions, but I know now that there are alternative ways of mitigating threatening moments.

When I turned thirty-five years old and quit my plum academic job to focus on motherhood, I retained my Harvard Medical School appointment as an Associate Professor of Psychiatry with no ambivalence. I wasn't sure what I was going to do next, but I knew I could no longer remain on staff at Beth Israel and continue to deal with patients in these barbaric ways. There were few places to refer seriously ill poor patients who had no support systems. As Susan Sheehan asked in her 1982 Pulitzer Prize-winning memoir *Is There No Place on Earth for Me?* became the question that eventually consumed me (Sheehan, 1982).

I gravitated toward the poverty world, initially working with unhoused families and their children and focusing on mental health issues, especially trauma. A few colleagues and I conducted qualitative research at the model state shelter for homeless men in Massachusetts. When I walked into the shelter, I felt like I was back at Boston State Hospital. It was readily evident that many of the residents were mentally ill. I was taken aback and wrote an article in *The American Journal of Psychiatry* about our findings entitled "Is Homelessness a Mental Health Problem?" (Bassuk et al., 1984). It was a naive and contentious article since I didn't yet understand the politics of homelessness. The advocates readily explained that if politicians could make homelessness a mental health problem and divert funding away from the unhoused, it would be harmful. In retrospect, I felt embarrassed by my limited understanding, but the experience launched me into the politics of the homeless world, and I learned that mental illness is a small but significant part of the poverty and housing problem—the root causes of homelessness.

Some years later, after conducting additional research on homelessness and spending time with people who were living on the streets, I gravitated toward the moms and their children. Seeing young mothers with most children younger than six years old who had no safe place to be at night troubled me—at the time I had two infants and had formed my own family and could barely imagine being in their desperate situations with little opportunity and options. What sad and scary circumstances for young children who constituted most individuals in homeless families. And how could a single mom fully protect her children in these circumstances?

In 1988, I founded and became the president of a non-profit organization initially called The Better Homes Fund and later the National Center on Family Homelessness—the first national organization solely devoted to families and children experiencing homelessness. My professional directions were not preordained or planned but seemed to follow my moral compass and beliefs, coupled with serendipity that provided me with some unexpected choices and essential resources, initially from *Better Homes and Gardens* magazine.

During this period, the primacy of traumatic events and their impact on brain functioning gradually emerged and helped to transform how doctors understood our patients. However, advances in brain science have not dramatically changed care protocols except in managing trauma and in the use of medications. The care of patients with serious mental illness has evolved far more slowly, except with increased attention to patients with first-episode psychosis (Murphy et al., 2015). Many of these people do not receive adequate care, although their disorders may be lifelong and disabling. Only recently have Recovery principles and systems of care helped change our damaging view of their outcomes as we have developed a renewed belief in their ability to have a fulfilling life of meaning and purpose in which managing symptoms is but a small part of their experience. These principles certainly influenced how we proceeded with Daniel's care.

Most of all, the changing nature of psychiatry inspired my choices. Psychiatry has been changed by the transformation of the health-care system into a highly technological big business, which further alienated me. A focus on revenue and profits has also grown. Some of these changes can be seen in the severe staffing shortages, closing of pediatric units—less lucrative than those for adults, shorthanded emergency rooms with very long waits, a decrease in overall bed capacity, the push by multi-billion dollar companies like CVS and Walmart to buy and invest in primary care practices, and the overall growth in private-equity investment in health care. Each day physicians are pressured into seeing more patients for shorter visits, and insurance reimbursements have become increasingly cumbersome, complex, and capricious because of a system that is more concerned with risk pools and the bottom line than with providing compassionate care.

With the changes in the system, the role of psychiatrists has gradually shifted as well, and they spend much of their time evaluating, diagnosing, and medicating patients and consulting with other specialists (Stein et al., 2022)—rather than treating them holistically with, for example, talk therapies (often combined with medications) such as cognitive behavioral treatment, trauma-specific treatments, and collaboration with health providers, which have been shown to be effective (Pellek, 2023). Instead, as dictated by insurers, many psychiatrists see patients briefly and intermittently rather than learning about and engaging deeply in their life circumstances as they did in previous years. A fifteen-minute monthly medication appointment, a common model, can't replace more intensive contact. Furthermore, despite the high prevalence of behavioral health disorders, especially among poor and vulnerable patients, many do not have adequate access to care and remain untreated. Health care disparities loom large, limiting access to quality medical care for many people. (Press, E. Standard of Care. *NYTimes Magazine* June 16, 2023. pp. 42–4.)

Over the years, since I first chose to specialize in psychiatry, many of my colleagues have moved away from providing talk therapies to solely prescribing and managing medication. Primary care has emerged over these years as the necessary first point of contact with patients, providing preventive care, diagnosis, and referral to specialists. As the health care system has changed, so has the role of primary care physicians who now also prescribe the majority of psychiatric medications to people with anxiety and depressive symptoms (Huo et al., 2023). The important exceptions are lithium and neuroleptics (which again highlight the difficulties treating people with serious mental illness) (Ivbijaro et al., 2014; Knaak et al., 2017). Given the changes in the health care system over the many years I have been a psychiatrist, and the changes in the ways psychiatric medication is prescribed, other models of care are being investigated that might relieve some shortcomings in the current system. Collaborative Care, an evidence-based model in which psychiatrists become consultants to primary care providers, is one of those approaches, but it has significant limitations (Insel, 2022). However, as one psychiatrist, Rachel Weir commented, "In my psychiatry clinic, I can see one patient in an hour, but using Collaborative Care, I can assist with the treatment of 10 to 12 patients in the same time . . . That's a very dramatic expansion of access" (Weiner, 2022).

Through research and many large-scale adaptations, consensus has identified four essential elements of Collaborative Care. These include the provision of care that is:

1) Team-driven
2) Population-focused
3) Measurement-guided
4) Evidence-based (American Psychiatric Association & Academy of Psychosomatic Medicine, 2016).

In other words, a multi-disciplinary group of health-care providers works as a team to provide high-quality evidence-based care to a defined population of patients. The study found that a mental health specialist such as a psychiatrist or psychiatric nurse significantly contributed to improved outcomes, but their diminished role has not been addressed.

The University of Washington AIMS Center (Advancing Integrated Mental Health Solutions) has designed, translated, and researched innovative approaches to integrating a Collaborative Care model for people with behavioral health problems, especially depression and anxiety (Aims Center, 2023a). The model is being disseminated in large health-care organizations such as the Veterans Administration and Kaiser Permanente, as well as in fee-for-service systems and federally funded clinic systems of care. By reviewing a vast literature, they describe how the collaborations of various health-care professionals and paraprofessionals—for example, a PCP, case manager (CM), and consulting psychiatrist—working together can improve the outcomes of people with depression and anxiety. They have not yet expanded this model to other mental health disorders. The PCP oversees the team, designs the patient care plan, and is the primary decision maker, while the CM ensures the linkages among providers, patient engagement, and adherence to the plan.

The psychiatrist acts as a consultant, reviewing the treatment plan and making necessary modifications. Their primary role is to clarify diagnoses and make medication recommendations.

Although the Collaborative Care Model includes psychiatrists, their overall role has changed, and they are now consultants both to the PCPs and the behavioral care managers. They are no longer the primary professional providing talk therapy, sometimes with medication, and getting to know their patients over time as they did decades ago. In fact, talk therapies combined with medication (when necessary) are not at the forefront of the profession as they were when I was a resident, and psychiatrists no longer have a distinct and singular role in treating patients with mental health disorders (Aims Center, 2023b).

Although these approaches address various systems issues, many PCPs are not experienced in the care of patients with mental disorders and generally do not provide ongoing talk therapies as psychiatrists might. They generally treat patients with minor to moderate anxiety and depression. Furthermore, few of the models described provide care to people with serious mental illness, especially schizophrenia (Loeb et al., 2012). Xavier Amador, former director of psychology at the New York State Psychiatric Institute, expresses an even more cynical, but perhaps accurate view of psychiatry. He states that "psychiatrists are no longer trained to look at someone's long-term needs. They've turned into mechanics, dispensing psychopharmacology over a 72-hour period . . . .and then, "My job is done" " (Amador, 2007).

Recent data supporting Amador's view indicate that the number of visits to a psychiatrist for therapy has dropped precipitously—by 50 percent between 1996 and 2016 (Fernández et al., 2021). The lowest rates were among those on Medicaid, persons labeled schizophrenic as well as Black people and Hispanics. Now, if they are available, psychologists, social workers, nurse practitioners, and peer specialists are relied on for talk therapies, but they do not have the medical or psychopharmacological expertise of psychiatrists (American Psychological Association, 2025).

In early 2024, the Centers for Medicare and Medicaid Services (CMS) announced a pilot project, Innovation in Behavioral Health Model (IBH). It is community-based and integrates physical health needs into behavioral health organizations and is slated to be implemented in eight states. It is focused on providing integrated physical and behavioral health care to Medicare and Medicaid populations that have moderate to severe mental health conditions and substance use disorders (SUD). These groups have largely been ignored and tend to have poor health outcomes, visit the ER often, and have high rates of hospitalizations. This pilot promotes integrated care, an interprofessional care team led by a behavioral health provider, health equity plans, and expanding health information technology. Its major goal is to address the unmet needs of a marginalized population with extensive health needs. Integration of care led by a psychiatrist modifies the Collaborative Care model and opens the door for reducing health disparities, especially among people with intense needs. Although its stated principles of care are Recovery based, we still don't know enough about its effectiveness and must learn more about how to care for people with serious mental health disorders (Centers for Medicare & Medicaid Services, 2024).

These findings raise the question of what the current role of psychiatry in our complex health care system should be. Psychiatrists have increasingly become medication dispensers and consultants to a multidisciplinary team. A growing percentage of talk therapy is now conducted by psychologists, social workers, nurse practitioners, and now certified peer specialists, a considerable portion via telemedicine. Overall, patients with psychoses, particularly schizophrenia and bipolar illness—the more serious and often life-long disorders—remain an enormous challenge and have not yet been adequately integrated. Comprehensive treatment of these extremely stigmatized subgroups must be moved to the forefront of the research and clinical agendas (Goodrich et al., 2013; Unützer et al., 2013; Whitebird et al., 2014). Recovery has also focused our attention on people with the most serious mental illnesses who have often been relegated to custodial institutions, the prison system, or the streets. However, we still need an evidence-based comprehensive toolkit and public support (and consequently government) to make their care a priority.

The role of psychiatry must be reevaluated and retooled—and psychiatrists' medical expertise fully valued. A Recovery approach—often part of how some psychiatrists interacted with patients—integrates individualized, person-centered care where the illness is viewed as only part of a person's experience—

should be revived. This approach eventually helped Daniel even as we figured it out on our own.

Given the changes in the field of psychiatry over my lifetime and the emergence of Recovery approaches, I wonder if, had they been available to Daniel earlier—the norm instead of an experiment—his course might have been different. In recalling the circumstances that contributed to the more troublesome events and acute precipitants of Daniel's psychiatric hospitalizations that began during adolescence, it is only now almost two decades later that I can make any sense of them. At the time, I was putting one foot in front of the other and trying to do my best for my children, obviously with some difficulty. I felt chronically overwhelmed, sad, fearful, and like a failure for not being able to control some of these outrageous and frightening experiences—the traumas of his childhood, his school expulsions, and his mistreatment or neglect by adults who were supposed to have his best interests at heart.

Daniel suffered, and I wonder how the external events contributed to his many diagnoses, bizarre symptoms, and growing disorganization. He clearly had a mental health disorder, but the circumstances of our lives made things worse—*how* much worse was impossible to know in the moment. At the time, my goal was survival and maximal protection of my children. I silently berated myself for not doing better and wondered what more I could accomplish. Somehow, though, I still believed things would improve. This conviction helped me persist in seeking every conceivable way to try to reduce the stress and improve their lives. Supports were minimal, even from my family, who had their own challenges, as well as people in my community who assumed our troubles were the norm for a family headed by a single mom with two complicated kids. And those supports would diminish further as things went from bad to worse.

Part III

Journey Back to Personhood

16

Tortuous Uphill Road

After Daniel started taking Clozaril (clozapine) and was discharged from High Point to his father's care on Cape Cod, he began to slowly emerge from the ravages of his psychotic illness. At first, he was unable to care for himself, organize his day, or communicate his needs and wishes. The voices were still tormenting him, and although he was more organized on Clozaril, he could barely function. There were times when the voices were so disturbing that he had to continue to resort to putting quarters in his ears and tinfoil on his head. We connected him to the local mental health agency, the department of mental health case managers, and a community mental health center. He also continued to see his psychiatrist at McLean Hospital in Boston.

Daniel improved but needed considerable support to function minimally. He stayed at his father's home until the fall of 2005 and then, as he improved ever so slightly, Daniel, who was now twenty-two, moved into his own apartment near his dad, although he often required sustained support to get through the day. He had two bedrooms and a large porch. He had some casual contact with his neighbors. He also had two snakes: one was a large blood python named Sophia; he often let her out to sun on the porch. The other was a boa constrictor that he eventually gave to a truck driver when she grew very big and aggressive.

The voices continued to dominate, telling him what to do, what to wear, and how to behave. They dictated where he should walk, often blocking his way so he was unable to move in a straight line. He avoided various places where the voices seemed to gather. Although the friendlier voices were present, they didn't protect him. LeRoy and Ed continued to torment him by touching him inappropriately. Leroy would try to kiss Daniel, and when he tried to stop him, Leroy would be more persistent and get angry. To get away from them, he would ride his bike or go to the gym. Despite the voices, Daniel created a lonely but purposeful life on the Cape.

> *While I was living at Cape Cod, I did lots of community service. I worked at kennels with rescue dogs, food dispensaries, a daytime psychiatric facility, and an aquarium. At the Woods Hole Aquarium I would rehab sick sea turtles. My job was to feed them. They were very big and weighed about 300 lbs. I would also clean the other fish enclosures. They even had me check the minnow traps that were by the docks to find anything interesting that could be on display at the aquarium. During the day at the aquarium kids came on school trips and would ask me a million questions and I was able to answer most of them. One other interesting thing is that at the aquarium the botanists gave a prosthetic eye to a common sea bass to make it more appealing for public display.*
>
> *I also worked for a year at the Marine Resource Center, a research facility, and would feed the sea creatures, such as toad fish, squid, and horseshoe crabs, and clean their enclosures.*

For a brief time, Daniel also had a paid job at the local garden center where he loaded trees using a forklift, sorted, watered, and fed plants. He worked there for five months, but sadly when the owner got sick, the place closed. Daniel's various jobs helped him focus, gave him a sense of purpose, and helped build his confidence and self-esteem, but he remained isolated and had no friends. He was too shy to reach out and talk to people. Except for his parents, the only person he talked to regularly was an older woman from India who he said was "crazy" and whose job was to prevent people from jumping off the Bourne Bridge connecting Cape Cod with the mainland. She had experienced something he described as "cast iron torture." He also began drinking alcohol, which later became a problem to be resolved. A group of kids tried to get him involved with drugs, but he only used marijuana four or five times.

Daniel's father became his major support during his time on the Cape. He helped him with all his daily activities, took him out to eat, and made sure he got to his appointments, including his regular biweekly visits to his therapist at McLean Hospital. Two healthcare workers helped out when Daniel needed additional support and his father was busy with work. Daniel remembers that they also went kayaking, swimming, went out to eat, and went to the gym; he enjoyed their company and the activities.

When Daniel was twenty-six years old, after living on Cape Cod for four years, he had exhausted the available mental health services that were critical to meeting his needs. It was time for him to move back to Boston where he could find a comprehensive treatment program. He was doing much better than in 2004, but still had considerable difficulty getting through the day, so we investigated potential programs in Boston as a vehicle for this transition and decided that the best fit was Boston University's Center for Psychosocial Rehabilitation, which had a clear recovery orientation.

> The Center for Psychiatric Rehabilitation is a research, training, and service organization dedicated to improving the lives of persons who have psychiatric disabilities… It is based on the belief that people with psychiatric problems have the same goals and dreams as other persons…

The staff had extensive experience working with people with serious mental health issues. Many had lived experience and provided peer support services. Founded by William Anthony, who is often referred to as the "Father of Psychiatric Rehabilitation," the Center's perspective on client care was unique, person-centered, and Recovery based (Gagne et al., 2007). They not only believed in support and maintenance but also in the importance of instilling hope about the possibility of having a fulfilling future.

Admission was a complex process because Daniel was continuing to struggle with internal preoccupations, including the voices and relating to other people. He was wary of any changes. When we first visited, he was worried about being in a program with people who looked mentally disabled and was anxious about anything new or different from his situation on the Cape. At the same time, he wanted to figure out if the Center could help him since he was so distressed and lonely. Despite his wishes to relieve his suffering, he was restless, uncommunicative, paranoid, agitated, and reluctant to get involved in even a brief conversation.

By March 2009, Daniel was somewhat more comfortable with the staff at the Center and agreed to visit a few times a week. The plan was to ease him into this new environment and begin to make some connections with staff and peers. During that summer, while still living on the Cape, he enrolled in Boston University's summer program. He initially had a tough time—not talking for hours, being internally preoccupied, and unable to relate to anyone or to actively participate in the program. But we persisted. After more time, considerable discussion, and Daniel's growing comfort at BU, he agreed to move to Boston, continue to participate at the center, and find a residential program where he could live.

> *In my early thirties I had some social anxiety. I was seeing my psychotherapist. I would often not go out for long periods of the day. I would be up to three hours late for my appointments as well as other obligations that were pressing. Some wondered if it was OCD, but it was due to social anxiety. I am learning to get over this as well as to get a handle on my voices. Having a cat named Samantha helped me get over my worries and anxiety. I then made it to my appointments on time.*

In January 2010, with considerable support, Daniel moved into an apartment at Side by Side Supported Living (SBS) where he lived until September 2013. SBS is located in a large old Brookline apartment building, with various units reserved for people participating in the program. It is near public transportation and accessible to shops, restaurants, and an array of stores. The building was unobtrusive and not vastly different from the adjacent apartments. Case managers and associated staff had offices in the basement, where the residents met for community meetings, group therapy sessions, and other relevant meetings. The residents would often gather informally in a community room. Daniel's apartment had one bedroom, a large living room, and a kitchen. It was a corner apartment on the second floor, and he relished both the privacy and the feeling of independence. Daniel brought his pets, which made him feel safer, including his cat Samantha, two large fish tanks, and Sophia, his python.

SBS provided an array of services for each client, including residential support, money management, and a wellness program. The residential support program included instruction in areas such as health and personal care, social development, assistance in the use of medications, implementation of a yearly individual support plan (ISP), case management, twenty-four-hour on-call supports, weekly menu planning and grocery shopping, hosting one dinner a week, and eating Friday and Sunday night dinners with other residents.

In addition to the SBS program, Daniel began seeing a psychotherapist and a psychiatrist who prescribed and monitored his medications—primarily 500 mg of Clozaril—which he had begun taking at High Point in 2004.

Daniel's transition into SBS brought additional difficulties that had been previously less apparent. His formal thought disorder—his voices—was less obvious at first but was still tormenting him and dictating his behavior. In addition, he had significant problems planning, organizing, following instructions, taking initiative, and regularly participating in program activities. His apartment was a mess. His dishes piled up in the sink, he was overeating, his dirty clothes were strewn all over the floor, and he had such difficulty maintaining his fish tanks that many of his fish died. His apartment was so dirty that the residents in adjacent apartments often complained of the smell that emanated from it. Despite prompting from the case managers, he had difficulty getting to dinners and group meetings at all or on time. The staff noted that he was listening to voices and was very preoccupied.

> According to Daniel the voices told him what to wear, and where to go. They wanted to put him in dangerous situations. Poltergeist come out of the sides of the T. They give him the finger and would swear at him. Daniel thinks they are trying to take his thoughts away from him (personal communication, April 14, 2010).

Daniel repeatedly asked to see his old doctor from McLean who might help him get rid of the voices, but his care was transferred to Dr. Cather in psychiatry at Solomon Carter Fuller Mental Health Center in downtown Boston. Over the first few months, the voices became even more persistent and told him that he had to drink and smoke more weed. He bitterly complained of their constant intrusion in his life and how noisy they were. Sometimes he increased the volume on his TV to try to block them out, but they just got louder. He felt he had no control in his life and everyone else dictated what he was supposed to be doing.

Daniel liked the taste of vodka and began drinking a few times a week. He said it helped him relax. At various times, he was found in front of the main SBS building very drunk. The staff talked to him repeatedly about the adverse effects of alcohol, especially when combined with Clozaril.

During this difficult period, he began cutting himself. He said it was to relieve his depression and despair, and to get the voices to stop torturing him. This combined with his drinking became difficult to manage. Sometimes, he would get so drunk he would urinate in the laundry room and sleep there. Once while on a binge, he was picked up by a trans woman who went up to his apartment and tried to steal his belongings, but the staff found her hiding in the closet and Daniel passed out on the floor. During this period, he had a serious cutting episode and was finally admitted to the substance abuse unit at Arbour Hospital. As Daniel said, "there was no more skin to cut." He was hospitalized for eight days and said that all he did was sit around. Over the next year, his doctor convinced him to attend group sessions focused on abstaining from alcohol and beginning the process of recovery. These groups were effective although Daniel didn't like going. There were many heroin addicts, and he was afraid of them. He decided the only way to get out of the groups was to quit drinking. He stopped using alcohol by the end of the year and has been sober ever since.

Daniel clearly needed more support if he was going to be able to live even partially independently and function in the community. Dr. Dori Hutchinson, now director of BU's Center, stepped in to support Daniel and implement a Recovery-oriented approach to his care that supplemented the strategies used at SBS. This represented the real beginning of his lengthy road back. In an email sent to me and the staff at SBS and at BU, Dr. Hutchinson emphasized,

> We have learned over the last 1.5 years that Daniel does best with structure. We cannot merely invite him to class or an activity as he is not always internally organized enough to execute on just our prompting and invitation to participate. Of course, this is the goal but at this time he still needs *elbow-to-elbow coaching.* When he leaves classes due to his symptoms, we have found that following him out and letting him know that sitting with him in class works very well.

She went on to explain why a Recovery-oriented approach was critical for his future development.

> We are also discovering that as his psychiatric treatment has improved through clinical services at MGH, he is emerging from his illness experience. Prior to his crisis (e.g., cutting), we all noticed that he never seemed so well. This has been a very painful awakening as his cutting indicated. We call this the 'rehabilitation crisis" here, when people begin to realize all the losses associated with living with severe mental illness and as a result feel even more hopeless despite having made improvements. This seems to be happening for Daniel. He is acutely aware of all that he doesn't have in his life right now and we feel that it has conspired in his recent self-injurious behavior.
>
> It represents a wonderful opportunity to engage him around his increased self-awareness through acknowledgement of all that he has gone through and lost, as well as hope that he can have the life he wants and that we will all work with him to help him build that life. He needs to be affirmed as a valued member of our communities. We hope to engage him socially with his peers in the young adult class. (D. Hutchinson, personal communication, c. 2012)

To further supplement services for Daniel, we hired more case managers, especially those with lived experience who were comfortable providing elbow-to-elbow coaching. We brought in Donna Wilbur, a peer specialist who met Daniel when he first went to the Center. She spent time with him looking at videos of small animals, and they initially made a real connection. It was as if they had known each other for a long time. They had common interests, and Daniel felt safe with her. She was a calm, competent, and kind case manager who worked closely with Daniel as a personal care assistant and continues to help him with the activities of daily living. She supplemented the SBS staff, who prompted Daniel primarily by phone but did not work with him more intensively. With Donna's aid, his self-care and organizational skills began to improve. As Daniel improved, Donna modified her role with him, helping him with organization and encouraging his forays into the community. Donna is a major support for Daniel now, more than fifteen years later, and is in contact with him almost every day.

Some of the other case managers, most of whom were peer specialists, worked well with him, but given the circumstances in their lives, they came and went. An exception is Suruchi, who is from Nepal and began working with him when she arrived in the United States. She now talks to him daily on the phone and gets together with him weekly. As Daniel has improved, her role has changed. She spends time with him developing better social skills, exploring employment options, and promoting organizational skills. Most importantly, they have developed a long-lasting, meaningful connection. Donna and Suruchi have become the backbone of Daniel's support network.

By the end of Daniel's first year at SBS, and with the help of the case managers, he gradually began to improve and create a more livable environment for himself and his pets. As he got used to SBS and settled into the routine, his treatment team arranged for him to do volunteer work. He started at Webster House, a clubhouse for people with mental health issues. He worked in the kitchen washing dishes, preparing food, and occasionally serving other residents. He had an aversion to being around people with obvious mental health difficulties and quit after three months.

With Donna's support, he volunteered at a cat shelter where they cleaned cages and brushed and played with the cats. He liked it enough to continue for six months. After that, he volunteered at the MSPCA walking dogs, cleaning cages, and washing dishes and laundry, but he was mostly interested in working with the more aggressive dogs. He managed to continue at MSPCA for almost a year and was viewed as a hard worker. These experiences helped him develop a work ethic and improve his sense of self-worth—showing up on time, relating to other people, completing tasks—and developing self-esteem and a sense of accomplishment.

More than anything else, Daniel wanted to be independent and no longer identified as a mental patient, as he had been for most of his life. He wanted to be like everyone else, to be in charge of his destiny and rid of the stigma that he had lived with since those early days at Montessori.

Unremittingly being a patient made him feel powerless and oppressed. He agitated to leave SBS and get his own apartment. Since we had many concerns about the fit between Daniel and SBS, and Daniel's treatment team was solidly in place, we agreed to look for an apartment that Daniel could live in that was in a neighborhood he was familiar with, where he felt safe and was close to transportation. Although he was still deeply troubled and the voices were highly active, with close supervision from the treatment team and reliable follow-through of his medication schedule, we thought it was safe to go ahead with a new plan.

> *I was at Side by Side (SBS) for almost three years. I left Side by Side knowing I would be better off on my own. I moved across the street to another building. I found more support by going to Boston's Center for Psych Rehab. Once living on my own, I did much better as I gained continued support from their program, felt safe, and liked living on my own in the community.*

This decision opened up a new and somewhat unknown chapter in Daniel's life that was initially dominated by his treatment team and other critical supports, his reliable use of his meds, and his inherent strengths and capabilities—and most of all his determined wish to be independent and a person living in community like the rest of us.

17

The Recovery Process

Almost two decades after Daniel's florid psychotic break, he has gradually regained himself and his life. The road to recovery has been neither easy nor linear. He suffered relentless setbacks and challenges. The seeds of difference and illness were sown from the time he was a baby, and the systems set up to help him seemed unable to respond adequately to his needs. Thankfully, there were exceptions, with some caretakers able to deal compassionately with his otherness. Fortunately, we were able to maintain some of the supports necessary to help him weather this challenging course. I never lost hope, although I had many moments of despair about his future, haunted by visions of my greatest fear coming true: placement in Bridgewater State Hospital—essentially locked up. We implemented a Recovery approach that included his move into the community, medication, continued connection to the center at BU, and most of all his stable treatment team, including his therapists and his parents, which has made all the difference.

> *Now I am in recovery, and I believe that living in my own apartment was just the push I needed to go all the way. I have many interests, and I had two jobs last year.*

The entire experience led me to consider what recovery truly is, especially for a serious mental illness. Definitions abound, but they overlap. The Substance Abuse and Mental Health Administration (SAMHSA) describes Recovery as "a process of change through which individuals improve their health and wellness, live a self-directed life, and strive to reach their full potential"

(Substance Abuse and Mental Health Services Administration, 2014). The Recovery movement emphasizes strengths and wellness, and the commonality of experiencing mental health challenges as a shared human process rather than an illness or deficit. Illness is only a part of the human experience. Hope is the catalyst, suggesting that everyone has the possibility of recovering and leading a more fulfilling life that gives them a sense of purpose. Managing symptoms and mitigating them is a goal—cure is not equivalent to Recovery.

The Recovery model views mental illness from a different perspective than traditional psychiatric approaches. The medical system has framed Recovery as returning to a premorbid level of functioning. As Larry Davidson described, the Recovery model rejects this framing, resting its priorities on the Recovery of the person with or without the disorder rather than the Recovery of the disorder *in* the person (Davidson et al., 2021). Instead of being illness-centered and deficit-oriented, this process is person-centered, and illness is only one part of each human's experience. Recovery promotes growth and is a lifelong process of discovery (Davidson et al., 2021).

As Davidson put it: "You can do it. We can help" (Davidson, 2016). The caretaker's role is to support the process, often through motivational interviewing, an evidence-based practice, where people find their way. The caretaker's role is also to support the individual's strengths and goals and to help them develop the confidence to move ahead in their lives (Treichler & Spaulding, 2017). Just as in Daniel's life, Recovery looks different for each person, which leads to different pathways.

According to SAMHSA, four major dimensions support a life in recovery: home, health, purpose, and community—with hope threaded through all of these and ongoing, engaged, compassionate, trusting relationships providing the anchor (Substance Abuse and Mental Health Services Administration, 2014).

So, how does Daniel's experience illustrate the process of recovery?

Home . . .

A critical dimension of Daniel's Recovery was his move from a residential program to his own apartment, where he has now lived for more than a decade. He takes immense pride in his independence, freedom, and having a place that he can call home, which is his own. His apartment is located near transportation, has a porch, and an extra room where he keeps his computer. Most importantly, it is a safe and stable environment where he lives with his beloved cat Clara and his two fifty-five-gallon fish tanks.

Health . . .

Conceptual changes in the understanding of behavioral health disorders have been a cornerstone of the Recovery movement and have helped Daniel immeasurably. Rather than focusing on problems and deficits, this movement places renewed emphasis on wellness and health, strengths, and the commonality of experiencing challenges as a shared human process. Recovery is holistic, encompassing every aspect of the individual's life. It is often referred to as "whole person care."

Daniel has worked hard to achieve a healthy lifestyle that now includes frequent exercise, sleeping regular hours, meditating regularly, and eating well-balanced meals. He is active and walks many miles around the city. Although he struggles with weight issues because of his psychiatric medications, he has figured out ways to manage them.

Daniel has achieved a sense of wellness despite the need for treatment. He takes meds regularly and engages in talk therapy. He no longer views himself as someone who is severely impaired, defined by his illness, and unable to function in the world.

Purpose . . .

Along with maintaining his own apartment, Daniel is involved in community service and describes it as the "highlight of my life. It gives me purpose and a way of helping to change the world for the better." Daniel has worked in soup kitchens, animal shelters, and daycare facilities for people with serious mental illness.

Daniel is also engaged in meaningful daily activities of his choice. They give him direction, routine, structure, and most importantly, a sense of purpose.

Unlike the isolation Daniel experienced throughout his childhood, he feels part of a community of people—not only his family but also the relationships he makes. Daniel takes photography courses, Reiki, and writing courses, goes to a dojo three times a week, and takes music lessons, playing the acoustic and electric guitars. Many of these courses are at Boston University's Center for Psychosocial Rehabilitation.

In contrast to his earlier years, he is successful, and his self-esteem and self-respect have soared. He is proud of himself and feels more confident, capable, and focused. He has become the "captain of his own ship," deciding the direction of his life. Joining in activities that he has chosen and being welcomed into various groups has given him a sense of self-worth, self-respect, and clear belonging and acceptance for who he is: a lovable person with many strengths and desirable qualities. According to Daniel, "These classes give me confidence and raise my self-esteem." He now has the luxury of dreaming about life's possibilities and considering different options for the future.

Community . . .

Recovery is supported through ongoing relationships—the cornerstone of widespread healthcare transformation. They may include family members, friends, peers, providers, faith groups, community members, and other allies. They all form vital support networks. As SAMHSA has indicated, these networks should offer support and encouragement, leading to a greater sense of personhood, belonging, empowerment, autonomy, and inclusion. It is essential that the stigma and discrimination associated with mental illness also be addressed. Stigma is associated with one of the major barriers to recovery, not only compromising individuals' feelings of self-worth but interfering with access to adequate services.

I have little doubt that our family's consistency and support from the time Daniel was a baby made a significant difference in the face of his serious mental illness. Even when the school staff insisted I was too enmeshed and should spend less time with him, and the police and doctors raised the question of what kind of mother I was, I believed in the importance of standing strong and supporting my son—no matter what. I wondered how the schools could even question the necessity of a consistent and stable environment for Daniel. The systems adhered to protocols and rarely accounted for the unique differences among individuals, especially those who presented with unusual behaviors. Furthermore, it seemed that not enough was understood about behavioral health, nor was it adequately integrated into the systems Daniel was embroiled in.

The treatment team we formed for Daniel has been anchored by case managers like Donna and Suruchi, generally not from the mental health system, who treated my son like a valuable and appealing person. These connections are the bedrock of his Recovery journey. He has had long-standing relationships with several members of the team. Donna, who started out with him as a peer specialist and is now a licensed social worker, has been with Daniel since SBS. When they first met at BU's Center for Psychosocial Rehabilitation, Daniel was not able to manage the routine activities of daily living, and Donna acted as his personal care assistant, but the relationship has grown as Daniel has become more adept at managing himself and his life, and Donna now supports his independence and freedom, serving as a coach, support, and anchor.

Daniel currently sees a therapist who is a social worker that talks with him about managing various challenges in his life, including the challenges of medication and the presence of the voices. She has worked with him to build his self-esteem and spends part of each session bolstering his self-worth by having Daniel teach her how to play the guitar. As Daniel says: "She is very responsive, keeps our discussions confidential, and is good at processing concerns he has about family issues." He looks forward to seeing her, and they have been meeting weekly for several years. Their discussions are reinforced by his case managers.

This has been supported by seeing psychiatrist Dr. Garrett weekly.

Dr. Garrett is empathetic, compassionate, and eccentric because he specializes in dealing with voices and their meaning. He suggests that the voices may even be spirits and that I am not crazy. He is trying to encourage me to become the center of my life and move the voices to the periphery, I like seeing him because he is open minded, transparent, and inquisitive and always allows me to drive the conversation.

Given the challenges of his childhood and adolescence and his exclusion from school, Daniel has struggled to form peer relationships. He has had a few friends along the way, but he is shy and has had limited social practice. His case managers help him learn additional social skills when dealing with peers, and he is slowly getting more comfortable making friends. He has become more at ease in group settings and is working on finding individual friends, especially a girlfriend.

In recent years, now that Daniel lives in his own apartment, he is a conscientious member of his neighborhood. An elderly woman who lives upstairs has had several strokes, and Daniel chats with her and helps her with groceries. Daniel empathizes, saying, "She wants to retain her independence." Another elderly couple lives next door, and the husband has memory problems and occasionally wanders off. Daniel helps find him, and the wife has been "emphatically grateful."

Daniel is attuned to other people's hardships and needs and generally responds with tremendous compassion. He is sweet and likable, although he tends to be quiet and shy and is often described as "a gentle giant." I have always done my best to actively support this aspect of his personality and take immense pride in what a kind person he is despite all the adversity he has had to overcome.

Along with home, health, purpose, and community, there's a fifth factor to consider: *medication*. In years past, schizophrenia was seen as a deteriorating illness. Its roots are genetic and biological, often requiring management with medication. Although understanding the complexity of how the brain works has progressed, it is still in its infancy. A revolutionary approach to the treatment of schizophrenia occurred with the introduction of chlorpromazine (Thorazine) in the 1950s. It was the first effective antipsychotic medication (i.e., neuroleptic), with others following. During the past decades, various classes of antipsychotic compounds have been synthesized. They may differ structurally from Thorazine, but they are pharmacologically and clinically similar. They revolutionized the care of patients with serious mental health problems, and medication became a mainstay of treatment. Rather than institutionalization as the preferred therapy, Thorazine helped to open the doors of mental hospitals and integrate patients into the community. Antipsychotic drugs became a mainstay in the treatment of schizophrenia and other psychotic disorders despite ongoing controversy about their efficacy over the long term, especially considering the adverse effects and risks (Okhuijsen-Pfeifer et al., 2018; Stępnicki et al., 2018; Whitaker, 2010).

Recently, a new group of drugs for the treatment of schizophrenia has been introduced: atypical or second-generation antipsychotics, of which Clozaril (Clozapine) is one of the best known. Clozaril, which Daniel takes, primarily affects dopamine pathways and, to a lesser degree, serotonin, and helps to improve behavior, thinking, and mood. The introduction of these neuroleptics has expanded therapeutic options. Some hoped that it would be the "magic bullet" that would "cure" schizophrenia. It has been remarkably effective in some patients with schizophrenia who have not responded to other medications. However, it has significant adverse effects, including sedation, weight gain, and most importantly, the potential for suppressing bone marrow production, leading to agranulocytosis, a potentially fatal condition. Introduced in 1989, its dissemination was limited by the seriousness of its effect on white cell production. Over time, it became clear that caution with the use of the drug, through monthly blood tests measuring white blood cells and Clozaril levels before another prescription can be refilled, increased its safety (De Berardis et al., 2018). Because of the possibility of serious adverse effects, the drug is tightly controlled, requiring monthly blood tests. It is a difficult drug to take long-term. However, Clozaril has made a dramatic difference in the lives of patients, including Daniel, but it is not the whole story or the magic bullet.

Consistent with SAMHSA's view of the factors that support recovery (2014), Daniel, with the help of his treatment team, has supported his health. Although he was initially and understandably resistant to taking the high dose of Clozaril that helped him, over time he somewhat reluctantly agreed on the importance of taking the medication regularly and has worked out a strategy for ensuring that he deals with his resistance and takes the meds daily. For several years, Daniel called me on FaceTime at exactly 8:25 PM every evening and had me watch him take his meds. He developed this strategy to be sure that he took the medication as prescribed and that the voices didn't derail him. As he has matured, this has become unnecessary, and he slowly stopped these calls. He takes his medicine regularly now on his own and is feeling more confident about relying on himself.

Daniel says that the medications "help me sleep, take the edge off the voices becoming unrelenting and prevent me from becoming slightly paranoid." However, that doesn't mean he doesn't complain about the need to get monthly blood tests, as well as tolerate the sedative effects and weight gain associated with the drug. As with other people with a diagnosis of schizophrenia, he at times has stopped the drug briefly and then experienced a re-emergence of some of the more troublesome symptoms of psychosis. He has chosen to take the meds regularly. Overall, the drug, combined with another relatively new drug called Abilify, has helped him immeasurably. According to Pat Deegan, who introduced "Empowerment Medicine" (Deegan, 2019),

> Learning to use psychiatric medicine optimally to support recovery is a dynamic journey. It requires more than learning to take pills on schedule. . . . Optimal use of medicine means finding that sweet spot where, on most days, using medicine to help manage mental health challenges fades into the background, and living life takes center stage. Optimal use means using the fewest medications at the lowest effective dose. It does not necessarily mean being symptom free. Instead, it means developing a set of self-care skills and supports to help manage and minimize mental health challenges. I call these skills "personal medicine." For many of us, finding the right balance between what we do (personal medicine) and what we take (pill medicine) is the pathway into the life we want for ourselves. . . . Additionally, optimal use means finding acceptable and livable trade-offs between the risks and benefits, side effects and desired effects, of medicine. (Deegan, 2020)

As I look back on Daniel's long and challenging recovery journey and the factors that have made a difference, it is informative and very encouraging to review where we have been and hopeful to see how far we have come. When asked about his life, Daniel described his childhood as "rough."

> *I feel I was dealt a lousy deck of cards. I had many diagnoses, many hospitalizations, and many therapists. Nothing really helped. I had few friends and was very lonely.*

Given his nightmarish experiences over so many years coupled with the ongoing presence of his community of spirits, I've puzzled over the factors that have contributed to his process of Recovery. Daniel is now an appealing, thoughtful young man with little outward evidence of the serious illness from which he suffers. In the early hours of the morning when I can't sleep, I ponder Daniel's remarkable course; I am grateful for his improvement. Although he lives with a parallel reality, he has managed the ways the voices can derail him and has figured out methods to contain their attempts at controlling him. It has also helped that as his strategies for coping have developed, some of the voices have receded. It has been encouraging to consider where Daniel has been and where he is going.

> *At first, I heard voices and believed everything they said, but then I learned that some of what they said wasn't real. I developed a thick skin and the voices' attempts to get me to do things that don't make sense such as rearranging my bookcase, I don't have to respond to and nothing awful will happen. I am the captain of my ship and can take the lead in my own life.*
>
> *I believe that the voices suggest something about the duality of one's cognitive functioning. Some voices being bad while most of them are good. It's all a misfiring of the brain. All we are is our brains. When we agree with our brain things go well. When we disagree with our brain things go bad. Things go bad in the sense that our subconscious is turned against us, thus resulting in schizophrenic behavior. Living with the voices has been a very confusing lifelong task. What one with schizophrenia is told at first becomes true for the patient at the end. I have lived with the voices evolving while I myself have mentally evolved as well. I am in good company now, with my voices that is. Every day or so I hear or see some of them. It's not*

bad at all now. They are still present and probably will be present for the rest of my life.

It is important to acknowledge that although Daniel has made remarkable progress, things are not always rosy. Daniel still must deal with the impact of his long history—school exclusion, more than ten hospitalizations, isolation and loneliness, managing his symptoms, and often feeling like a pariah.

How do I feel about my life? What is my view of the world, given my ten hospitalizations? I feel stigmatized. I feel judged. I feel forgotten about. I feel all of it was major setback after setback, to the point moving on is unlikely. I will never have a normal life like other people. I am too late for things like marriage, college, and being successful. I fear what people think of me because it matters to me. I fear people think I am a psycho…and perhaps I was.

I worry about what will happen when I am older. I feel the mental health system has done its best to help me, but it lacks the funding and understanding to help everyone. The mental health system is difficult to improve. What we need to do is keep going with what works and throw out what does not, replacing it with new ideas that must be exercised under scrutiny. The future is not set. There is hope. Random acts of kindness are everywhere.

Similar issues apply to the Recovery movement. Just as Daniel continues to deal with various challenges and develop and grow, so does our understanding and implementation of recovery. The systems that are in place to support Recovery remain a critical part of an individual's journey. Recovery also focuses on the need to redesign services that are more person-centered and responsive to individual needs, with shared decision-making used to empower patients. Services are most effective when providers understand what recovery is, believe it is possible, work to develop trust, and are caring and compassionate as they meet people where they are" (Hunter, 2018).

As part of the service redesign, peer support services must be center stage. Peer relationships are especially powerful since they model Recovery and illustrate that people with mental illness can have productive, fulfilling lives. They help to instill and sustain a hopeful perspective. Considerable work must be done to successfully integrate Recovery principles, including peer support workers, into health care settings, including educating caretakers and staff, developing person-centered protocols, providing adequate training and supervision, and addressing stigma, implicit bias, and structural racism.

Donald Berwick, a renowned health policy analyst, further defines person-centeredness as "the experience of transparency, individualism, recognition, respect, dignity, and choice in all matters without exception, related to one's person, circumstances, and relationships in healthcare" (Berwick, 2014). He identifies three dimensions (Berwick, 2014, p. 131):

1. The needs of the person come first.
2. Nothing about me without me.
3. Every patient is the only patient.

Recovery-oriented principles of care must be applied to all the systems caring for people with mental illness. This is a tall order. As time has passed, Recovery approaches have become increasingly embedded within critical systems of care. As these issues have become more connected to the major issues of our times, such as human rights and the many layers of racial equity, the structural factors contributing to the poor quality of mental health care, coupled with bed and staffing shortages, are being exposed, paving the way for ongoing systems reform.

18

Real People, Real Empathy, Real Connection

As a mom and as a psychiatrist, it seemed that the major factors contributing to Daniel's Recovery are in some ways mysterious, but a combination of them made a major difference: the ineffable effect of time, the intrinsic nature of his illness which is largely unknown, carefully selected medications, talk therapy, engagement in many meaningful activities in which he succeeded, living independently, his parents' commitment, and most important, the formation and ongoing involvement of the treatment team that largely consists of people who are Recovery-oriented and able to see Daniel as a person. As Daniel's experience shows us, Recovery does not occur in the hospital. Recovery begins outside the hospital. "Nothing about us without us," as James Charlton wrote. The term "expresses the conviction of people with disabilities that they know best what is best for them" (Charlton, 1998). The creation, evolution, and impact of the treatment team and its central importance in Daniel's Recovery journey over his lifetime reflect the blueprint we organically developed to address his needs.

Daniel improved steadily when he began living independently. It bolstered his confidence and self-esteem. But it began before that. During adolescence, when Daniel was homeschooled, his main case managers were a college student from El Salvador who had grown up in South Central Los Angeles and a young man who had just graduated from college and was planning on teaching ESL in Cambodia. They saw Daniel as a kid struggling to grow up—a whole person. We layered our own treatment team on top of the traditional mental health professionals who continued to deal with Daniel in a formulaic manner. This strategy was built on our belief in the importance of Daniel establishing continuous, trusting relationships with people who knew him well and saw him as a growing boy, not a label.

We continued this approach when Daniel was living at Side by Side. Donna was key—she was the first regular member of the "independent living" treatment team; she supported Daniel's transition from residential living to relative autonomy. Once Daniel was living in his own apartment, she initially helped him organize his life, but most importantly she became an abiding presence that grounded him.

The SBS staff generally prompted Daniel to complete his daily tasks but did not provide the elbow-to-elbow care he required, nor did they form anchoring relationships to ground him and make him feel safe. Donna did this. She also shared her lived experience with Daniel—giving him hope about his future and the possibility of having a fulfilling life and not always being viewed as "the mental patient."

During and after he left SBS, along with Donna, some of his social workers took a genuine interest in Daniel and formed peer-like relationships. They were close in age and interested in music and the world of spirits. We gradually added people, including Suruchi, to the treatment team as Daniel grew more independent. She was warm and initially arranged many activities for Daniel. She introduced him to peers and helped him with some of the college courses he later took. At the time of this writing, she is working with him on developing additional social skills, still talks to him every evening, and meets with him regularly. As with all his case managers, she understands the consequence of establishing a relationship on Daniel's terms and encourages him to set his own course. Shared decision making is central to their approach.

These long-standing connected relationships continue to be critical for Daniel's ongoing growth. Engaging him in an authentic relationship was done cautiously and accompanied by clear limits and boundaries, followed by structured meetings. The case managers do not move too quickly and ensure that Daniel's decisions are made in collaboration with them and that he is actively participating in the process. They encourage him to set concrete, clear, and practical targets. Since Daniel's current goals are related to jobs, school, friends, and dating, they focus their energies in these areas. For example, a major goal was to volunteer taking care of animals, so they helped Daniel sign up for work at a cat shelter cleaning cages, washing bedding, and grooming cats. Another goal was to support Daniel in getting to his appointments on time. These goals are not dictated; they are determined by Daniel, and their implementation is actively supported by the team. They try to ensure that outcomes are readily achievable, like attending a social event or having a meaningful conversation. He has accomplished many of these goals.

This did not happen overnight. It took some time for Daniel to settle into his apartment and for the treatment team to get their bearings. At first, the focus was on working out a regular routine that Daniel accepted and could accomplish. Over the next few months, with the support of the treatment team, he became more able to follow through on many of the activities of daily living—regular grocery shopping, doing his laundry, preparing some of his meals, and feeding his cat. He also became increasingly active. He walked to the boxing gym, which was a few miles away, and worked out several times a week. He went for long solitary strolls around the neighborhood, sometimes even going into downtown Boston to eat Chinese food.

During this period, he continued to hear voices, but with the help of his therapists, he was more able to figure out ways to manage them. Since they emerged, the voices have tended to fluctuate, and the so-called "bad ones"—Leroy, Ed, and William—reappearing now and then. Daniel's relationship with them has changed over time. He has learned to avoid listening to what they tell him to do. He says that he feels less powerless in their presence, especially given his success at the part-time jobs he has had.

Not long after Daniel moved into his own apartment, he started taking his medications sporadically and, when not closely supervised, not at all. Independent living meant to Daniel that he was fine enough, and he no longer needed them. Clozaril is a difficult drug to take regularly. Daniel had significant adverse effects, including severe sedation, weight gain, and constipation. Because Clozaril is a controlled substance, he had to get monthly blood tests before he could refill his next prescription. Given these challenges, Daniel resisted taking the meds and stopped them periodically. Predictably, he became symptomatic with worsening hallucinations, paranoia, and agitation that interfered with his ability to function. When this occurred, he would guard against the voices by putting tin foil in his baseball cap, keeping people out of his apartment, and fearfully avoiding the police. Antipsychotic meds for some people with mental illness result in a cruel trade-off, but Daniel has no life without them and now takes them volitionally.

Medication is but one example of how the treatment team worked hard with Daniel and gradually adjusted to his changing needs. As he began to function better and was able to do more, we fine-tuned the structure of the team. We added a team leader who had both administrative and supervisory functions and ensured that team members were on the same page and conveying consistent messages to Daniel. It was important that expectations of Daniel were clear, practical, and uniform. The team leader was also the point person whom the team members and I trusted and who was the designated person who communicated with me, Daniel's father, and consulting providers—and maintained clear and acceptable boundaries. For many months, the team met weekly and included his therapist, team leader, and case managers. Daniel was empowered to run the meetings, and he liked the attention and the positive feedback. He discussed how the week went and raised any concerns such as keeping his apartment organized and clean, and his objections to being in the substance abuse groups. The team reinforced his positive behaviors and gently suggested areas that need improvement. Over time, the configuration of the team changed, and as Daniel has grown even more, the formal weekly team meetings were abandoned.

Currently, the major focus is on socialization—supporting him to engage with people and make new connections. This is supported in no small way by his continued involvement with BU's Center for Psychosocial Rehabilitation. A letter from Dr. Hutchinson provides a concrete account of Daniel's improvement and is markedly different from the assessments he received when he was younger.

> I have known Daniel Schoonover for several years since he first attended classes here at Boston University Center for Psychiatric Rehabilitation. Over those years, I have witnessed remarkable changes happening for Dan.

When Daniel was beginning his time here with us, he was clearly having difficulty connecting with the program, the teachers, and the other students. He would frequently arrive late for classes and leave early, sometimes only staying for a few minutes before making his exit. His body language was either defensive or conflicted, and his eye contact was sporadic. I believe that Daniel was having to deal with a great deal of internal dialogue and "hearing voices." As time passed, Daniel would take breaks from classes and then return now and then. Most recently, Daniel was showing enormous signs of behavioral improvement. Daniel would sign up for classes, come to our Tai Chi class, arrive on time, and stay for the whole class, during which he was often the only student who had questions. It was clear to me that Daniel was also doing some homework, which is rare for students with a diagnosis of a serious mental illness. Daniel has reached out to staff, teachers, and other students alike, attempting to make contact and build relationships. These last behaviors make for an extremely positive and a "remarkable" change for Dan.

What are the characteristics of the treatment team that made it so successful and promoted Daniel's remarkable growth? Most importantly, the members were empathic, problem-solved together, listened to and validated Daniel's experiences, and saw him as a *whole person, not an illness.* Daniel was included as a primary team member, and unlike many of his previous experiences, his voice was valued. He felt heard and supported. The team responded with concrete, practical messages that were helpful to Daniel. The composition of the team also supported his growth. The team members came from different disciplines and perspectives, including education, social work, psych rehabilitation, psychology, and psychiatry. Donna, as a therapeutic mentor with lived experience and now a licensed social worker, openly talked with Daniel about her complicated road to recovery and that recovery was possible regardless of the illness. She showed him the way and was only steps ahead of him.

When Daniel was having more difficulty, the team met both with him and each other to coordinate care and form a trusting partnership providing what Dr. Hutchinson called elbow-to-elbow care. As he has moved on in his life, the formal team meetings have been abandoned. The team now consists of two case managers who together address approaches to supporting him. They have telephone and in-person contact with him multiple times a week. Further supporting these activities are his therapist (supportive social worker) and psychiatrists who prescribe medication and submit a requestion for his monthly blood test and Clozaril level. These relationships have greatly increased his self-esteem. When Dr. Garrett was added to the team, Daniel benefited greatly from his help with the management of his voices.

Although the team is now smaller, it remains a critical part of Daniel's recovery and ongoing search for a sense of purpose and meaning in his life. Regardless of the direction, he continues to seek activities that validate his choices. Unlike the years he spent trapped in the mental health system, he has developed a sense of freedom and self-worth that has encouraged him to continue exploring life's possibilities with enthusiasm.

In the past five years I have been doing well living on my own. I have been taking classes at BU. My favorite classes have been music with an acoustic guitar, photography, beekeeping, poetry, recovery classes, and working at the women's lunch place. All these activities have helped me to do better. I like all kinds of music particularly the blues. I have been keeping up with all my chores and participating in all the forementioned activities. It's nice to be on my own. I have more independence. I have no specific goals for the future, but I am thinking hard about what they might be. I have a lot of choices. I want more education. It's never too late for that. I feel I have benefited from all the things I am doing. I plan on taking more classes at BU and continuing with karate. I am close to receiving a black belt. I am even taking a course on herpetology and hope to get certified.. The case managers have been very supportive.

19

Glimmers of Purpose and Hope

From the beginning of Daniel's journey through the lost years of his childhood, the ravages of his severe mental illness, the appearance of the community of spirits, to his steady emergence back to personhood and to independence and a self-directed life, we have raised questions about the impact of the systems around him. Our story is embedded in a discussion of their limitations and a call for their redesign based on person-oriented, trauma-informed Recovery principles—*Daniel as a human with hopes, dreams, and wishes—not an illness.*

We also specifically focused on the changes and consequent limitations of the mental health system and its flawed efforts to serve people with serious mental illness. As a psychiatrist and parent of a child diagnosed with mental health problems, I have traveled through medical, educational, and criminal justice systems for many years, bearing witness to a steady regression from humanistic caregiving to impersonal, high-tech responses that generally disregard an understanding and honoring of an individual's unique needs, capabilities, wishes, and humanity.

Daniel's experience reflects just that. It is a cautionary tale of how misunderstanding, labeling, inattention to a person's experience, and at times lack of empathy and compassion may contribute to unnecessary suffering and adverse outcomes. From the age of three, Daniel was excluded from almost every school, treatment program, or activity because of his differences, disability, and the associated stigma. Saddled with half a dozen diagnoses, many of his providers implemented interventions doomed to failure by their limited understanding of him, not addressing the multiple traumatic stresses he experienced, the increasing rigidity of the system, and the influence of the insurance companies. After most standard responses had failed, we worked relentlessly, drawing our own blueprint to create a custom recovery-oriented support system tailored to Daniel's unique needs. Led by his treatment team that we gradually designed and modified, their approach was anchored in empowering, respectful, and enduring human relationships, and driven by Daniel's choices, wishes, and hopes about his future.

> *The help I get from my treatment team has helped me in many ways. Donna has supported me for 15 years and I can count on her to always be there. I can tell her anything and she doesn't judge me. She is a great listener, and I see her every week. Suruchi has been by my side for more than seven years. She has encouraged me to move forward and to safely move out in the world. We went all over Boston and explored new places that I had never seen. She has taught me more social skills so I can be part of the community. She is also helping me to make friends and has broadened my horizons. My therapist is there too for the last 10 years—always supportive, accepting and listening closely. I feel very lucky to have these many people committed to me. And my new therapist has talked openly with me about my voices—a first.*

Another key piece in the puzzle is adding psychiatrist Dr. Michael Garrett to the treatment team. Most psychiatrists provide support to psychotic patients primarily with medication but do not provide ongoing talk therapy that helps them feel seen and understand their internal experience—Dr. Garrett is an exception and has written about how he integrates cognitive behavioral therapy with psychodynamic therapy for people labeled psychotic (Garrett, 2019).

> *A very special doctor named Dr. Michael Garrett has been able to help me quite extensively. His insight goes way beyond other doctors. He believes that the voices I hear are spirits, or my imagination brimming over, or both. We have talked a lot about my experiences with the voices I hear. He recommends books for me to read. He has played a very big part in my Recovery. He has*

read the draft of the book my mom and I are publishing and was impressed. He has more insight compared to other doctors I have met. Although almost every doctor I have met has been helpful in some way, Dr Garrett is semi-retired but luckily agreed to see me recently to talk about the voices. He called my voices a 'community of spirits' and I believe he is right about that. I believe he has helped a lot of people with the knowledge he has. He had me test the voices to see if what they say is true. I agreed to do that, and it has proven the voices should have no credibility with me based on what they say. This is a load off my shoulders. I've begun to understand how the voices represent aspects of my personality, my imagination has brimmed over, and my subconscious is talking. I still hear the voices and experience visual hallucinations, but I pay way less attention to them.

Dr. Garrett has made a remarkable difference in Daniel's understanding of himself and has buoyed his self-esteem. He has understood Daniel's perceptions, helped him understand them, avoided labels, and humanized his experiences. At no point has he lapsed into jargon or discussions that do not directly validate Daniel. Daniel feels more "normal," as he describes it to me, and sees his unusual experiences as just part of being human. What a difference from other therapies! With the entire team in place, he has been able to continue to move forward and fashion a life of creativity, curiosity, and accomplishment. Most of all, Daniel is now an independent young man who has many unusual talents and interests, a real capacity for empathy and connection to the animals and people around him, and an intuitive compassion for those less fortunate. He is continuously working on managing his symptoms, living with his voices, and learning that they are part of him, reflecting aspects of who he is. Most importantly, he has learned that he is not his illness, and he is eagerly exploring options for the future. His Recovery journey continues, and he is hopeful.

Integrating Recovery strategies into the health care system and putting principles into action is a formidable task. When our medical, educational, and criminal justice systems are ready to acknowledge and embrace the transformative potential of personal empowerment and human connections,

I hope that Daniel's success will become the norm, as will that of many, many others. However, transforming systems that deal with people who have mental health issues is daunting. It would be easy to make a laundry list of supports and activities to reduce stigma and change practices, but it is unlikely that it would make a meaningful difference. Many educational campaigns, for example, have been developed to address discrimination against people who are different by reason of race/ethnicity, gender, sexual orientation, and disabilities. Most observers would agree their outcomes have been equivocal. Attitudes are deeply entrenched; implicit bias is rampant, and stigma occurs at individual and systemic levels. Furthermore, converting feelings into action is a challenging task, especially within complex and highly technological systems that have become big business.

Any type of systems transformation can only occur incrementally. Instead of approaching mental health care as a monolith, we must break the necessary changes into small pieces—and address them one at a time, issue by issue—as we enlist different sectors in this task. The medical system and the insurance companies are too entrenched, interconnected, vast, and driven by profit. If each person and each family adopts some of the Recovery principles, changes may occur over time. As described by neurosurgeon Myron L. Rolle, when addressing issues of systemic racism, "We need to decide that we are going to move the needle ever so slightly, every day. By reading more, by advancing policy, by communicating . . . we can break the mold," and facilitate the process of change by "applying the 2% way" (Rolle, 2022a, 2022b). Incremental change is the goal in the healthcare system as well. Change will only occur if each person, their families, and major supports commit themselves to critically important changes. Over time, these incremental changes will accrue and multiply and will begin to crack the current embedded structures. As Daniel's evolution shows, this is already starting to occur. There is reason to be hopeful, but the road is a long one.

The principles and values inherent in the Recovery model offer clues about strategies that might contribute to change. Daniel and I have tried to highlight the major principles underlying the Recovery model. Care is centered on the whole person and is eclectic, flexible, and changeable in response to patients' needs and wishes. Continuous, trusting relationships anchor the system.

Most importantly, people seeking services rather than providers control their own care, and their needs, values, and goals are respected. We also must acknowledge the limitations of the biomedical model and include in our thinking the significant role of environmental issues, especially psychological stresses, trauma, and adverse childhood experiences, as well as cultural issues in the etiology of mental illness.

Addressing the interdependence of class, gender, race/ethnicity, and collective intergenerational trauma may also may greatly influence outcomes. Trust in the road to Recovery is anchored by sturdy connections.

There is no single way to ensure a child's outcome. I am not suggesting that our interventions become the specific road to Recovery but rather a general blueprint for change that each family adapts to their own circumstances; the Recovery principles of care are universal, but the path has to be uniquely modified for the needs of each child and family. Daniel and I were fortunate enough to have resources and the room to explore alternatives, yet the road was still long and tortuous. But if each family adopts a Recovery approach, sticks to it, and adapts what is possible, and if they have enough energy to participate in some educational and advocacy activities, changes may slowly occur. Without a doubt, the resource question is a challenging one because of how underfunded the system is and how anyone with limited resources (especially insurance) is adversely affected.

Hope remains the catalyst for parents with children who are different. No matter how challenging one's circumstances, the belief that nothing remains the same and that positive change is possible will help to motivate sustained action. Although the road is challenging, painful at times, and different from many of your peers, it is well worth it. As parents, our key role is to love and protect our children, to help our kids create a life of purpose and meaning, to help them manage their symptoms, and to see the illness as only one part of their experience.

As much as possible, entering and accepting a child's inner world is a critical early step. With Daniel, it took many years before he felt safe enough to share some of his internal experiences, especially concerning the voices. He was far more open about how self-defeated he felt and how hurtful it was to be seen as so different from his peers. As he matured, we were able to discuss the meaning and place of his diagnosis of schizophrenia, of which he was so shamefully aware. We always tried to clarify that he is not schizophrenia but instead was Daniel, a young man struggling to fit in but still retaining strengths and capabilities. We tried to focus on the attainability of his hopes and dreams, which for so long he only reluctantly expressed. As Pat Deegan emphasizes, we must support their voice and choices and work through the challenges to help them "get the life they want." This was fortified by seeking out peer specialists who can model hope and fulfilling lives and who have lived experience. Donna's successful life course, for example, has been a wonderful role model for Daniel despite the early challenges she faced. This relationship also helps to keep his hopes and dreams active and attainable.

The mental health care system can be overwhelming, unresponsive, and intimidating. When consulting a doctor or other mental health provider, trust yourself and don't hesitate to ask questions and stay informed, especially about the effects of medications, but remain aware of the likelihood of implicit biases about mental illness. If you feel unheard, mobilize more support. Whenever possible, choose Recovery-oriented providers. Although caring for a person with serious mental illness can be draining, mobilize whatever energy you have to get involved in advocacy efforts and be in contact with legislators who support Recovery-oriented mental health policies and pay attention to the structural shortcomings of the system. Join mental health organizations, (e.g.,NAMI) as well as advocacy groups. Stay on top of current proposed legislation. Write to your legislators and hold them accountable.

First-person stories are often effective in influencing people. Use these in your advocacy efforts. See Recovery approaches as an asset in the struggle to modify discriminatory attitudes and systems. Find Recovery-oriented support systems, including peer specialists, to help in your efforts and willingness to use your experiences to help modify attitudes and reduce implicit biases.

In addition to what we can do, various critical changes must also be made now in the *current* system of care so that the principles of Recovery begin to infiltrate the system more fully and are adopted by providers, and all people are provided with high-quality care, especially in psychiatric inpatient settings. Wellness and recovery should become a priority rather than a singular focus on acute care. Adequate supports must be available and accessible to ensure that we can begin to overcome the stigma associated with mental illness.

An important direction is to retool psychiatry, bringing it back to its earlier humanistic roots, integrating our growing knowledge base and focusing on prevention and Recovery. Psychiatry is generally defined as "the medical specialty devoted to the diagnosis, prevention, and treatment of mental disorders," yet, with the exception of the introduction of medication along with rehabilitation and community-based programs, which are underfunded and scarce, not enough has changed since Kennedy announced his "bold new approach." Prevention and recovery, compassionate and person-centered care anchored by long-term relationships, have been eclipsed by a focus on the description of disorders and diagnoses—not on outcomes. The biomedical model prevails, often at the expense of compassionate patient-centered care. This must change (Insel, 2022).

To accomplish these changes, adequate education and supervision about mental health must be provided. Most difficult is figuring out how to address the deep divide for people living in poverty as well as those from diverse cultural and ethnic backgrounds. Intersectionality, or as defined in the OED, "the interconnected nature of social categorizations such as race, class, and gender, regarded as creating overlapping and *interdependent* systems of discrimination or disadvantage," must be considered. For example, racial equity is necessary to ensure health equity (Oxford English Dictionary, n.d.).

This realignment and deeper understanding provide a framework for redesigning the American healthcare system. This shift is best embodied by the principles of Recovery-oriented person-centered care, an age-old approach to high quality, compassionate care. As Epstein and Street in "The Values and Value of Patient-Centered Care" remind us: "The originators of client-centered and patient-centered health care were well aware of the moral implications of their work, which was based on deep respect for patients as unique living beings and the obligation to care for them on their own terms" (Epstein & Street, 2011). Daniel's experience from the time he was a toddler to now a man of forty dramatically illustrates how implementing Recovery-oriented strategies anchored by empathic relationships promotes healing and helps a person regain his humanity and self-respect.

Over my many years as a psychiatrist, I have witnessed the art of medicine becoming the business of medicine, and the values I cherished falling away. As a doctor and single mother, I navigated the thoroughly intertwined medical and educational labyrinths and even brushed up against the criminal justice system; all of which, in their own ways, have changed from humanistic and person-oriented to hyper-efficient, high-technology businesses in which honoring an individual's humanity and unique experiences has taken a back seat. It's not just diagnosis, but everything from racial profiling to educational testing to two-dimensional telemedicine to the power of insurers to make healthcare decisions. *Naming something does not fix it.* This evolution has especially affected anyone who is different: people like my son, Daniel, whose serious mental health issues coincided with these developments.

Even though this book focuses primarily on Recovery-oriented care, the broader health care system must also change along with changes in the care of patients with mental health issues. President Biden in his 2022 State of the Union Address laid out a blueprint for some of these changes. Among the changes he suggested were addressing severe staffing and bed shortages, increasing presence in areas of greatest need, building a national certification program for peer specialists, and expanding the ability of community programs to provide evidence-based services. Political will, adequate funding, and ongoing advocacy efforts both within psychiatry and from the broader population are necessary to "foster a culture and environment that promotes mental wellness and Recovery" ("2022 State of the Union Address," 2025). After all, the crisis in mental health is not a medical one but a societal one" (Insel, 2022) "and a measure of the soul of our nation" (Insel, 2022, p. 242). "What matters is not only what Washington does but what each of us do at home" (Insel, 2022, p. 242). We all must work to ensure change.

Daniel and I hope our story will inform everyone dealing with otherness and help to mitigate stigma and misinformation about mental illness. We wrote this book for parents, educators, caretakers, healthcare providers, policymakers, people with and without lived experience, and those of diverse cultures and races. Although there is an egregious disparity—people with more resources have more options—the quality of care is substandard for everyone. Most of all, we hope that those who are part of the caretaking systems will embrace the principles in this book, particularly by promoting a journey of Recovery, based upon person-centered and trauma-informed care, and the wishes, dreams, and hopes of each individual.

> *Even though my future is not certain, I am content with how things seem to be going for me. As long as I have compassion and empathy things will likely work out. Life is too short. My greatest pleasure other than my love for this earth is to eventually help others. When will the day come that I "Pay it forward"? I am grateful for all the help I have received during my troubled childhood and young adulthood. I have support from people when I need it. I am almost 40 years old, which is why I want to help people's lives to get better before I get too old. I just have to keep moving forward. I want to make all the difference I can before I leave this earth because what I do to better this life for other people will hopefully still be in effect long after I am gone.*

In closing, Daniel's hopes and dreams are eloquently presented in this poem he wrote one night as he was thinking about what he had endured and how he could continue moving toward a life of meaning and purpose.

> *The sun is shining yellow golden light over the beautiful land.*
> *A land once ruled by kings who were pure of heart*
> *But their kindness is not forgotten*
> *the clouds float by resembling peaceful thought*
> *Thoughts of happiness last forever*
> *Through an angel's eye kind deeds are everywhere*
> *Such kindness fills the heart with white light*
> *Full are the sails of joy*
> *Selfless acts of pure purpose cause great peace*
> *The reuniting of long-lost friends is a blessing*
> *Forever speaking, no, shouting the truth*
> *the truth being constructed with tranquility*

Acknowledgments

This book was a labor of love, inspired by my children's complex recovery journeys. It evolved naturally from my decades of parenting those who were othered. I never thought I would write something so personal or partner with my son, Daniel, in the process. It was both a wonderful and painful experience—especially hearing and validating his perspectives, watching him grow, and seeing him willing to describe his view of what happened to him and how he felt.

The major background materials for this book sat in a big box in my basement for nearly two decades. I had kept all the reports, consultations, school and medical records, and testing results from the time Daniel was a toddler. I spent most of a year sorting through the vast collection of information and discovering what these materials revealed from his early years. It was a difficult process, but Daniel and I were able to examine the events from many perspectives besides our own—his teachers, aides, consultants, physicians, therapists, case managers, and other written records—and incorporate pertinent sections into this book.

Many people worked hard with Daniel and were committed to his growth, and I am deeply grateful. James Keefe, a behavioral school consultant, was a major support in the early years, always responsive and present when Daniel needed him. His elementary school teachers, especially Virginia Watkins and Martha Harrington, acknowledged his struggles and remained committed to him. When he began homeschooling at age eleven, Hester Brooks helped Daniel become computer savvy, and of course, Jim Keefe continued to be there. We also began to sow the seeds of a treatment team—initially including case managers Albert Jovel and Aaron Reed—who saw Daniel as a boy struggling to grow up and tame his demons. A special thank you to them both.

Dori Hutchinson, Psy.D., the current director of Boston University's Center for Psychosocial Rehabilitation, has been an anchor and advisor at key points. The formation, evolution, and changes in our treatment team have been critical to Daniel's recovery journey. When Daniel was at Side by Side, he was floridly psychotic and unable to carry out daily activities. Dr. Hutchinson introduced us to Donna Wilbur, who remains the heart of Daniel's treatment team. Now a licensed social worker, Donna's lived experience allowed her to connect with Daniel authentically. She initially served as his personal care assistant, but her role has evolved with Daniel's growth. Fourteen years later, she remains devoted to him, staying in touch with him most days and providing him the security of knowing that, in addition to his parents, someone is always there for him. Similarly, Suruchi Khand has been dedicated to Daniel for almost a decade, speaking with him five nights a week. We are profoundly grateful.

Various mental health therapists have guided Daniel through many difficult times, bolstering his confidence, encouraging him to share his experiences, and offering immense support. Special thanks to Miles Cunningham, Michael Cauley, Corrine Cather, Jamie Freed, David Golden, and Michael Garrett. A particular thank you to Dr. Garrett for his transformative work with Daniel and for generously reading a draft of this book, providing comments that challenged me to rethink my views on psychiatry.

As Daniel's parent, I received support from so many people, and I want to acknowledge them all. I can only list a few, some of whom have since passed, but each made my life less stressful at different times: John Mack, Nancy Avery, Stas Gavronsky, Pilar Jennings, Lenore Rubin, Jayne Samuda, Joan Rook, Julie Santoes, John Kellogg, Amy Salomon, Sarah Minden, Kristen Paquette, Livia and Steve Davis, Rose Clervil, Barbara Raives, Sean Person, Aaron Reed, and Dawn Moses.

Many others helped transform our experiences with the healthcare, educational, and criminal justice systems into this book. Most of all, a heartfelt thank you to Alice Peck for being my editor, literary maven, and patient friend. She provided critical feedback, helped shape the book's structure, and remained committed to the process. Her knowledge, kindness, sage advice, skilled editing, and hard work improved it immeasurably.

Thank you to Tim Hayes, Daniel's and my literary agent, who believed in this book and was relentless in his pursuit of publication. His encouraging words, warmth, and ongoing support made a difference.

Gratitude as well to my editors and the production team at Bloomsbury, especially Sarah Rinehart, to graphic designer Duane Stapp, and especially to artist Matthew Ducharme who helped make Daniel's voices visible.

I am also grateful to my family, friends, and colleagues who encouraged Daniel and me, read drafts at various stages, and provided invaluable feedback. Maria Mutch read an early version and offered astute comments and suggestions as did Tanya Frank. Adam Koplan was involved early on as well, always helping me take the next step. His historical knowledge of our family helped refine many chapters. A special thank you to my sisters Susan and Janie and to Andre, who read and commented on the manuscript.

Most of all, we are grateful for all the people who remain part of Daniel's remarkable recovery journey and provide continuing support to his family.

References

2022 State of the Union Address. (2025, February 1). In *Wikipedia*. https://en.wikipedia.org/wiki/2022_State_of_the_Union_Address#:~:text=Biden's%20speech%20was%20primarily%20focused,the%20economy%2C%20and%20social%20issues

Aims Center. (2023a). *About collaborative care*. Aims Center. https://aims.uw.edu/collaborative-care/

Aims Center. (2023b). *Primary care provider*. Aims Center. https://aims.uw.edu/team-structure/primary-care-provider-pcp/#:~:text=Overview%20of%20the%20PCP's%20Role%20in%20Collaborative%20Care%20(CoCM)&text=Within%20CoCM%2C%20the%20PCP%20directs,Health%20Care%20Manager%20(BHCM).

Alexander, M. (2020). *The new Jim Crow: Mass incarceration in the age of colorblindness* (10th ed.). New Press.

Alpert, B. (2015, July 31). New Cedric Richmond bill targets 'modern day torture' of solitary confinement. *Times-Picayune*. https://www.nola.com/news/politics/new-cedric-richmond-bill-targets-modern-day-torture-of-solitary-confinement/article_d12bf103-45ad-5602-9d9f-c2763aa94c9b.html

Amador, X. F. (2007). *I am not sick, I don't need help! How to help someone with mental illness accept treatment*. Vida Press.

American Psychiatric Association & Academy of Psychosomatic Medicine. (2016). *Dissemination of integrated care within adult primary care settings*. https://www.psychiatry.org/File%20Library/Psychiatrists/Practice/Professional-Topics/Integrated-Care/APA-APM-Dissemination-Integrated-Care-Report.pdf

American Psychiatric Association. (2013). *Diagnostic and statistical manual of mental disorders* (5th ed.). https://doi.org/10.1176/appi.books.9780890425596

American Psychological Association. (2025). *What is the difference between psychologists, psychiatrists, and social workers?*. Clinical Practice Guideline for the Treatment of Posttraumatic Stress Disorder. https://www.apa.org/ptsd-guideline/patients-and-families/psychotherapy-professionals#:~:text=Psychiatrists%20attend%20medical%20school%20and,years%20of%20full%2Dtime%20internship.

Baker, D. B., & Benjamin, L. T., Jr. (2005). Creating a profession: The National Institute of Mental Health and the training of psychologists, 1946–1954. In W. E. Pickren, Jr. & S. F. Schneider (Eds.), *Psychology and the National Institute of Mental Health: A historical analysis of science, practice, and policy* (pp. 181–207). American Psychological Association. https://doi.org/10.1037/10931-006

Ban, T. A. (2007). Fifty years chlorpromazine: A historical perspective. *Neuropsychiatric Disease and Treatment*, *3*(4), 495–500.

Barish, R. A., McGauly, P. L., & Arnold, T. C. (2012). Emergency room crowding: A marker of hospital health. *Transactions of the American Clinical and Climatological Association, 123*, 304–311.

Bartlett, J. (2022, September 29). Staffing shortages keep one fifth of psychiatric beds out of commission. *Boston Globe.* https://www.bostonglobe.com/2022/09/28/metro/staffing-shortages-keep-one-fifth-psychiatric-beds-out-commission/

Bassuk, E. L., Buckner, J. C., Weinreb, L. F., Browne, A., Bassuk, S. S, Dawson, R., & Perloff, J. N. (1997). Homelessness in female-headed families: Childhood and adult risk and protective factors. *American Journal of Public Health, 87*, 241–248.

Bassuk, E. L., & Gerson, S. (1978). Deinstitutionalization and mental health services. *AMHC Forum, 31*(2), 39–46.

Bassuk, E. L., Richard, M. K., & Tsertsvadze, A. (2015). The prevalence of mental illness in homeless children: A systematic review and meta-analysis. *Journal of the American Academy of Child and Adolescent Psychiatry, 54*(2), 86–96.e2. https://doi.org/10.1016/j.jaac.2014.11.008

Bassuk, E. L., Rubin, L., & Lauriat, A. (1984). Is homelessness a mental health problem?. *The American Journal of Psychiatry, 141*(12), 1546–1550. https://doi.org/10.1176/ajp.141.12.1546

Bassuk, E. L., Weinreb L., & Buckner, J. C. (1996). The characteristics and needs of sheltered homeless and low- income housed mothers. *Journal of the American Medical Association, 276*, 640–647.

Bateson, G., Jackson, D. D., Haley, J., & Weakland, J. (1956), Toward a theory of schizophrenia. *Behavioral Science, 1*, 251–264. https://doi.org/10.1002/bs.3830010402

Bennet, A., & Schiller, L. (1996). *The quiet room: A journey out of the torment of madness.* Grand Central Publishing.

Berwick, D. M. (2014). *Promising care: How we can rescue health care by improving it.* Jossey-Bass.

Blair, R. D. (2012). Temporal lobe epilepsy semiology. *Epilepsy Research and Treatment, 2012*, 751510. https://doi.org/10.1155/2012/751510

Burke, N. J., Hellman, J. L., Scott, B. G., Weems, C. F., & Carrion, V. G. (2011). The impact of adverse childhood experiences on an urban pediatric population. *Child Abuse & Neglect, 35*(6), 408–413. https://doi.org/10.1016/j.chiabu.2011.02.006

Carlson, E. T., & Simpson, M. M. (1964). The definition of mental illness: Benjamin Rush (1745–1813). *The American Journal of Psychiatry, 121*, 209–214. https://doi.org/10.1176/ajp.121.3.209

Carr, E. R. (2024). A history of the community mental health movement and individuals with serious mental illness: A vision for the future. *The American Journal of Orthopsychiatry, 94*(4), 380–391. https://doi.org/10.1037/ort0000737

Center for Psychiatric Rehabilitation. (n.d.). *About us*. Boston University. Retrieved February 13, 2025, from https://cpr.bu.edu/about/

Centers for Disease Control and Prevention. (2024, May 15). *Data and statistics on Tourette Syndrome.* Tourette Syndrome. https://www.cdc.gov/tourette-syndrome/data/index.html

Centers for Medicare & Medicaid Services. (2024). *Innovation in Behavioral Health (IBH) Model.* Innovation Models. https://www.cms.gov/priorities/innovation/innovation-models/innovation-behavioral-health-ibh-model

Charlton, J. I. (1998). *Nothing about us without us: Disability oppression and empowerment* (1st ed.). University of California Press.

Community Mental Health Act. (2024, February 20). In *Wikipedia.* https://en.wikipedia.org/wiki/Community_Mental_Health_Act

Coward, H. (1979). Mysticism in the analytical psychology of Carl Jung and the yoga psychology of Patañjali: A comparative study. *Philosophy East and West, 29*(3), 323–336. https://doi.org/10.2307/1398935

Davidson, L. (2016). The recovery movement: Implications for mental health care and enabling people to participate fully in life. *Health Affairs, 35*(6), 1091–1097. https://doi.org/10.1377/hlthaff.2016.0153

Davidson, L., Rowe, M., DiLeo, P., Bellamy, C., & Delphin-Rittmon, M. (2021). Recovery-oriented systems of care: A perspective on the past, present, and future. *Alcohol Research: Current Reviews, 41*(1), 09. https://doi.org/10.35946/arcr.v41.1.09

De Berardis, D., Rapini, G., Olivieri, L., Di Nicola, D., Tomasetti, C., Valchera, A., Fornaro, M., Di Fabio, F., Perna, G., Di Nicola, M., Serafini, G., Carano, A., Pompili, M., Vellante, F., Orsolini, L., Martinotti, G., & Di Giannantonio, M. (2018). Safety of antipsychotics for the treatment of schizophrenia: A focus on the adverse effects of clozapine. *Therapeutic Advances in Drug Safety, 9*(5), 237–256. https://doi.org/10.1177/2042098618756261

Deegan, P. E. (1996). *Recovery and the conspiracy of hope.* [Conference presentation]. The Sixth Annual Mental Health Services Conference of Australia and New Zealand, Brisbane, Australia. http://akmhcweb.org/recovery/deegan-recovery-hope.pdf

Deegan P. E. (2020). The Journey to use medication optimally to support recovery. *Psychiatric Services (Washington, D.C.), 71*(4), 401–402. https://doi.org/10.1176/appi.ps.201900506

Deegan, P. E., & Stiles, A. (2019). *Pat Deegan's personal medicine for distressing voices: A CommonGround guide.* Pat Deegan, PhD & Associates LLC.

DeParle, J. (2024, December 27). Migrants and end of Covid restrictions fuel jump in homelessness. *The New York Times.* https://www.nytimes.com/2024/12/27/us/homelessness-hit-record-level-in-2024.html

Dorothea L. Dix, *On Behalf of the Insane Poor: Selected Reports* (New York: Arno Press, 1971).

Dort, M., Strelow, A., Schwinger, M., & Christiansen, H. (2020). What teachers think and know about ADHD: Validation of the ADHD-school-expectation questionnaire (ASE). *International Journal of Disability, Development and Education, 69*(6), 1905–1918. https://doi.org/10.1080/1034912X.2020.1843142

Earley, P. (2007). *Crazy: A father's search through America's mental health madness.* Penguin Publishing Group.

Ebert, A., & Bär, K. J. (2010). Emil Kraepelin: A pioneer of scientific understanding of psychiatry and psychopharmacology. *Indian Journal of Psychiatry, 52*(2), 191–192. https://doi.org/10.4103/0019-5545.64591

Eghigian, G. (Ed.). (2009). *From madness to mental health: Psychiatric disorder and its treatment in Western Civilization.* Rutgers University Press.

Eikos. (2025, February). All Biz. Retrieved February 9, 2025. https://www.allbiz.com/business/eikos_1a-617-787-0001

Elliott, B., Joyce, E., & Shorvon, S. (2009). Delusions, illusions and hallucinations in epilepsy: 1. Elementary phenomena. *Epilepsy Research, 85*(2–3), 162–171. https://doi.org/10.1016/j.eplepsyres.2009.03.018

Epstein, R. M., & Street, R. L., Jr (2011). The values and value of patient-centered care. *Annals of Family Medicine, 9*(2), 100–103. https://doi.org/10.1370/afm.1239

Fay, S. (2022). *Pathological: The true story of six misdiagnoses.* HarperCollins.

Felitti, V. J., Anda, R. F., Nordenberg, D., Williamson, D. F., Spitz, A. M., Edwards, V., Koss, M. P., & Marks, J. S. (1998). Relationship of childhood abuse and household dysfunction to many of the leading causes of death in adults. The Adverse Childhood Experiences (ACE) Study. *American Journal of Preventive Medicine, 14*(4), 245–258. https://doi.org/10.1016/s0749-3797(98)00017-8

Fernández, D., Vigo, D., Sampson, N. A., Hwang, I., Aguilar-Gaxiola, S., Al-Hamzawi, A. O., Alonso, J., Andrade, L. H., Bromet, E. J., de Girolamo, G., de Jonge, P., Florescu, S., Gureje, O., Hinkov, H., Hu, C., Karam, E. G., Karam, G., Kawakami, N., Kiejna, A., Kovess-Masfety, V., … Haro, J. M. (2021). Patterns of care and dropout rates from outpatient mental healthcare in low-, middle- and high-income countries from the World Health Organization's World Mental Health Survey Initiative. *Psychological Medicine, 51*(12), 2104–2116. https://doi.org/10.1017/S0033291720000884

Fisher, J. (2017). *Healing the fragmented selves of trauma survivors: Overcoming internal self-alienation.* Routledge.

Fittipaldi, S. E. (1989). Human consciousness and the Christian mystic. In R. S. Valle & R. von Eckartsberg (Eds.), *Metaphors of consciousness.* Springer. https://doi.org/10.1007/978-1-4613-3802-4_16

Foot, J. (2015). *The man who closed the asylums: Franco Basaglia and the revolution in mental health care.* Verso Books.

Fuller, D. A., Sinclair, E., Geller, J., Quanbeck, C., & Snook, J. (2016). *Going, going, gone: Trends and consequences of eliminating state psychiatric beds.* Treatment Advocacy Center. https://www.tac.org/wp-content/uploads/2023/11/Going-Going-Gone.pdf

Fuller, T. (1988). *Nowhere to go. The tragic odyssey of the homeless mentally ill.* Harper and Row.

Gagne, C., White, W., & Anthony, W. A. (2007). Recovery: A common vision for the fields of mental health and addictions. *Psychiatric Rehabilitation Journal, 31*(1), 32–37. https://doi.org/10.2975/31.1.2007.32.37

Galińska-Skok, B., & Waszkiewicz, N. (2022). Markers of Schizophrenia-A critical narrative update. *Journal of Clinical Medicine, 11*(14), 3964. https://doi.org/10.3390/jcm11143964

Garety, P. A. (2001). Making sense of voices: By M. Romme & S. Escher. *The Psychiatrist, 25*, 406–407. https://doi.org/10.1192/pb.25.10.406-a

Garrett, M. (2019). *Psychotherapy for psychosis: Integrating cognitive-behavioral and psychodynamic treatment.* Guilford Publications.

Gawande, A. (2014). *Being mortal: Medicine and what matters in the end.* Henry Holt & Co.

Gilbert, L. K., Breiding, M. J., Merrick, M. T., Thompson, W. W., Ford, D. C., Dhingra, S. S., & Parks, S. E. (2015). Childhood adversity and adult chronic disease: An update from ten states and the District of Columbia, 2010. *American Journal of Preventive Medicine, 48*(3), 345–349. https://doi.org/10.1016/j.amepre.2014.09.006

Goffman, E. (1963). *Stigma: Notes on the management of spoiled identity.* Prentice-Hall.

Goffman, E. (2007). Asylums: Essays on the social situation of mental patients and other inmates (1st ed.). Routledge. https://doi.org/10.4324/9781351327763

Goodrich, D. E., Kilbourne, A. M., Nord, K. M., & Bauer, M. S. (2013). Mental health collaborative care and its role in primary care settings. *Current Psychiatry Reports, 15*(8), 383. https://doi.org/10.1007/s11920-013-0383-2

Grinker, R. R. (2021). *Nobody's normal.* W. W. Norton & Company, Inc.

Grob, G. N. (1994). *The mad among us: A history of the care of America's mentally ill.* Free Press.

Hamm, J. A., Rutherford, S., Wiesepape, C. N., & Lysaker, P. N. (2020). Community mental health practice in the United States: Past, present and future. *Consortium Psychiatricum, 1*(2), 7–13. https://doi.org/10.17650/2712-7672-2020-1-2-7-13

Harris, N. B. (2023, April 29). *Adverse childhood experiences and toxic stress* [Conference presentation]. Breaking Barriers Conference, Burlington, VT.

Hartwell, C. E. (1996). The schizophrenogenic mother concept in American psychiatry. *Psychiatry, 59*(3), 274–297.

Hearing Voices Network. (2024). *Welcome.* Home. https://www.hearing-voices.org/#content

Herman, J. L. (2022). *Trauma and recovery: The aftermath of violence—From domestic abuse to political Terror.* Basic Books.

Herman, J. L. (2023). *Truth and repair: How trauma survivors envision justice.* Basic Books.

Hogan, M. (2003 November) Recommendations to transform mental health care in America. *Psychiatric Services, 54*(11), 1467–1474.

Howe, I. (1976). *World of our fathers.* Bantam Books, 1976.

Hunter, N. (2018). *Trauma and madness in mental health services.* Palgrave Macmillan.

Huo, S., Bruckner, T. A., Xiong, G. L., Cooper, E., Wade, A., Neikrug, A. B., Gagliardi, J. P., & McCarron, R. (2023). Antidepressant prescription behavior among primary care clinician providers after an interprofessional primary care psychiatric training program. *Administration and Policy in Mental Health, 50*(6), 926–935. https://doi.org/10.1007/s10488-023-01290-x

Insel, T. R. (2022). *Healing: Our path from mental illness to mental health.* Penguin Publishing Group.

Institute of Medicine Committee on Quality of Health Care in America. (2001). *Crossing the quality chasm: A new health system for the 21st century.* National Academies Press (US).

International Mental Health Collaborating Network. (n.d.) *History of the recovery movement.* Our History of Mental Health. https://imhcn.org/bibliography/history-of-mental-health/history-of-recovery-movement/

Ivbijaro, G. O., Enum, Y., Khan, A. A., Lam, S. S., & Gabzdyl, A. (2014). Collaborative care: Models for treatment of patients with complex medical-psychiatric conditions. *Current Psychiatry Reports, 16*(11), 506. https://doi.org/10.1007/s11920-014-0506-4

Jablensky, A. (2010). The diagnostic concept of schizophrenia: Its history, evolution, and future prospects. *Dialogues in Clinical Neuroscience, 12*(3), 271–287. https://doi.org/10.31887/DCNS.2010.12.3/ajablensky

Jones, S. R., & Fernyhough, C. (2008). Talking back to the spirits: The voices and visions of Emanuel Swedenborg. *History of the Human Sciences, 21*(1), 1–31. https://doi.org/10.1177/0952695107086138

Kakar, S. (1992). Ramakrishna and the mystical experience. *The Annual of Psychoanalysis, 20*, 215–234.

Kleimaker, A., Kleimaker, M., Bäumer, T., Beste, C., & Münchau, A. (2020). Gilles de la Tourette Syndrome—A disorder of action-perception integration. *Frontiers in Neurology*, 11, 597898. https://doi.org/10.3389/fneur.2020.597898

Knaak, S., Mantler, E., & Szeto, A. (2017). Mental illness-related stigma in healthcare: Barriers to access and care and evidence-based solutions. *Healthcare Management Forum, 30*(2), 111–116. https://doi.org/10.1177/0840470416679413

Lifeline Center for Child Development. (2021). *Our programs*. https://www.lifelinecenter.org/our-programs

Lochner, C., Hemmings, S. M., Kinnear, C. J., Niehaus, D. J., Nel, D. G., Corfield, V. A., Moolman-Smook, J. C., Seedat, S., & Stein, D. J. (2005). Cluster analysis of obsessive-compulsive spectrum disorders in patients with obsessive-compulsive disorder: Clinical and genetic correlates. *Comprehensive Psychiatry, 46*(1), 14–19.

Loeb, D. F., Bayliss, E. A., Binswanger, I. A., Candrian, C., & deGruy, F. V. (2012). Primary care physician perceptions on caring for complex patients with medical and mental illness. *Journal of General Internal Medicine, 27*(8), 945–952. https://doi.org/10.1007/s11606-012-2005-9

Longden, E. (2017). Listening to the voices people hear: Auditory hallucinations beyond a diagnostic framework. *Journal of Humanistic Psychology, 57*(6), 573–601. https://doi.org/10.1177/0022167817696838

Longden, E., Read, J., & Dillon, J. (2018). Assessing the impact and effectiveness of Hearing Voices Network self-help groups. *Community Mental Health Journal, 54*(2), 184–188. https://doi.org/10.1007/s10597-017-0148-1

Lukoff, D. (1985). The diagnosis of mystical experiences with psychotic features. *The Journal of Transpersonal Psychology*, 17(2), 155–181.

Mack, John E. (2010) *Passport to the Cosmos*. White Crow Books.

McCutcheon, R. A., Reis Marques, T., & Howes, O. D. (2020). Schizophrenia-An overview. *JAMA Psychiatry, 77*(2), 201–210. https://doi.org/10.1001/jamapsychiatry.2019.3360

McGuire, T. G., & Miranda, J. (2008). New evidence regarding racial and ethnic disparities in mental health: Policy implications. *Health Affairs (Project Hope), 27*(2), 393–403. https://doi.org/10.1377/hlthaff.27.2.393

McLean: Child & Teen Mental Health. (2025). *Pathways Academy*. McClean Hospital. https://www.mcleanhospital.org/treatment/pathways-academy

Moskowitz, A., Dorahy, M. J., & Schafer, I. (Eds.). (2019). *Psychosis, trauma, and dissociation: Evolving perspectives on severe psychopathology* (2nd ed.). Wiley Blackwell.

Mueser, K. T., Rosenberg, S. D., & Rosenberg, H. (2009). *Treatment of posttraumatic stress disorder in special populations*. American Psychological Association.

Murphy, B. (2021, September 29). *Women in medical schools: Dig into the latest record-breaking numbers*. AMA. https://www.ama-assn.org/education/medical-school-diversity/women-medical-schools-dig-latest-record-breaking-numbers

Murphy, S. M., Irving, C. B., Adams, C. E., & Waqar, M. (2015). Crisis intervention for people with severe mental illnesses. *The Cochrane Database of Systematic Reviews, 2015*(12), CD001087. https://doi.org/10.1002/14651858.CD001087.pub5

Myers, N. L. (2010). Culture, stress and recovery from schizophrenia: Lessons from the field for global mental health. *Culture, Medicine and Psychiatry*, *34*(3), 500–528. https://doi.org/10.1007/s11013-010-9186-7

Nani, A., & Cavanna, A. E. (2019). Gilles de la Tourette syndrome: An overview. *Archives of Medicine and Health Sciences, 7*, 277–283.

National Alliance on Mental Illness. (n.d.) *The doctor is out*. https://www.nami.org/support-education/publications-reports/public-policy-reports/the-doctor-is-out/#:~:text=Nearly%20half%20of%20the%2060,when%20they%20need%20it%20most

National Alliance on Mental Illness. (n.d). *Facts & statistics*. https://namica.org/what-is-mental-illness/facts-statistics/

National Center for Health Workforce Analysis. (2022). *Workforce projections*. Health Resources & Services Administration. https://data.hrsa.gov/topics/health-workforce/workforce-projections

National Institute of Mental Health. (2022). *Recovery after an initial schizophrenia episode*. Research Funded by NIMH. https://www.nimh.nih.gov/research/research-funded-by-nimh/research-initiatives/recovery-after-an-initial-schizophrenia-episode-raise

National Institute of Mental Health. (n.d.). *Schizophrenia*. Mental Health Information. https://www.nimh.nih.gov/health/statistics/schizophrenia

National Scientific Council on the Developing Child (2007). *The timing and quality of early experiences combine to shape brain architecture: Working Paper #5*. http://www.developingchild.net

Nellis, A. (2024, May 2021). *Mass incarceration trends*. Sentencing Project. https://www.sentencingproject.org/reports/mass-incarceration-trends/

Novotny, M., Valis, M., & Klimova, B. (2018). Tourette syndrome: A mini-review. *Frontiers in Neurology*, *9*, 139.

Ragins, M. (2021). *Journeys beyond the frontier: A rebellious guide to psychosis and other extraordinary experiences*. Independently Published.

Okhuijsen-Pfeifer, C., Huijsman, E. A. H., Hasan, A., Sommer, I. E. C., Leucht, S., Kahn, R. S., & Luykx, J. J. (2018). Clozapine as a first- or second-line treatment in schizophrenia: a systematic review and meta-analysis. *Acta Psychiatrica Scandinavica*, *138*(4), 281–288. https://doi.org/10.1111/acps.12954

Ovsiew, F., & Munich, R. L. (Eds.). (2008). *Principles of inpatient psychiatry*. Lippincott, Wiliams, & Wilkins.

Oxford English Dictionary. (n.d.). Intersectionality. In *Oxford English Dictionary*. Retrieved February 2, 2025. https://www.oed.com/dictionary/intersectionality_n?tl=true

Pale of Settlement. (2025, January 29). In *Wikipedia.* https://en.wikipedia.org/wiki/Pale_of_Settlement

Patel, K. R., Cherian, J., Gohil, K., & Atkinson, D. (2014). Schizophrenia: overview and treatment options. *P & T: A Peer-Reviewed Journal for Formulary Management, 39*(9), 638–645.

Pellek, A. (2023, June 2). *The benefits of combined pharmacology and psychotherapy.* MedCentral. https://www.medcentral.com/behavioral-mental/cbt/the-benefits-of-combined-pharmacology-and-psychotherapy

Penn Medicine. (2017). *Dr. Benjamin Rush: "Father of American psychiatry."* History of Pennsylvania Hospital. https://www.uphs.upenn.edu/paharc/features/brush.html

Penney, D., & Stastny, P. (2008). *The lives they left behind: Suitcases from a state hospital attic.* Bellevue Literary Press.

Peterson, A. L. (2021). *A brief history of stigma: Looking for ways to move beyond mental illness stigma.* Mental Health @ Home Books.

Pinel, P. (1983). *A treatise on insanity: In which are contained the principles of a new and more practical nosology of maniacal disorders.* Classics of Medicine Library.

Public Schools of Brookline. (2025). *High school programs.* The Public Schools of Brookline. https://www.brookline.k12.ma.us/Page/2231#:~:text=Winthrop%20House%2C%20an%20off%2Dsite,some%20adolescents%20experience%20in%20school

Ragins, M. (2021). *Journeys beyond the frontier: A rebellious guide to psychosis and other extraordinary experiences.* Independently Published.

Ringer, N. (2019). Living with ADHD: A meta-synthesis review of qualitative research on children's experiences and understanding of their ADHD. *International Journal of Disability, Development and Education, 67*(2), 208–224. https://doi.org/10.1080/1034912X.2019.1596226

Rolle, M. L. (2022a, February 22). Apply the 2% way to systemic racism. *The Boston Globe.* https://www.bostonglobe.com/2022/02/22/opinion/apply-2-way-systemic-racism/

Rolle, M. L. (2022b). *The 2% way: How a philosophy of small improvements took me to Oxford, the NFL, and neurosurgery.* Zondervan.

Russell, D. (2018). *My mysterious son: A life-changing passage between schizophrenia and shamanism.* Simon and Schuster.

Rybakowski J. K. (2019). 120th anniversary of the Kraepelinian dichotomy of psychiatric disorders. *Current Psychiatry Reports, 21*(8), 65. https://doi.org/10.1007/s11920-019-1048-6

Sacks, O. (2013). *Hallucinations.* Knopf Doubleday Publishing Group.

Saks, E. R. (2008). *The center cannot hold: My journey through madness.* Grand Central Publishing.

Sayal, K., Prasad, V., Daley, D., Ford, T., & Coghill, D. (2018). ADHD in children and young people: prevalence, care pathways, and service provision. *The Lancet. Psychiatry, 5*(2), 175–186. https://doi.org/10.1016/S2215-0366(17)30167-0

Seeman, M.V. (2016). Schizophrenogenic mother. In J. Lebow, A. Chambers, & D. Breunlin (Eds.), *Encyclopedia of couple and family therapy.* Springer. https://doi.org/10.1007/978-3-319-15877-8_482-1

Shatz, D., Waxman, C. I., & Diament, N. J. (Eds.). (1997). *Tikkun Olam: Social responsibility in Jewish thought and law.* Jason Aronson, Inc.

Sheehan, S. (1982). *Is there no place on earth for me?* Houghton Mifflin Harcourt.

Simon, J. B. (2006). Perceptions of the IEP requirement. *Teacher Education and Special Education, 29*(4), 225–235. https://doi.org/10.1177/088840640602900403

Singh, A., Yeh, C. J., Verma, N., & Das, A. K. (2015). Overview of Attention Deficit Hyperactivity Disorder in young children. *Health Psychology Research, 3*(2), 2115. https://doi.org/10.4081/hpr.2015.2115

Smith, J. R. (2022). *Difficult: Mothering challenging adult children through conflict and change.* Rowman & Littlefield.

Solitary Watch. (2025). *Solitary confinement in the United States: The Facts.* Solitary Watch. https://solitarywatch.org/facts/faq/

Stein, D. J., Costa, D. L. C., Lochner, C., Miguel, E. C., Reddy, Y. C. J., Shavitt, R. G., van den Heuvel, O. A., & Simpson, H. B. (2019). Obsessive-compulsive disorder. *Nature Reviews. Disease Primers, 5*(1), 52. https://doi.org/10.1038/s41572-019-0102-3

Stein, D. J., Shoptaw, S. J., Vigo, D. V., Lund, C., Cuijpers, P., Bantjes, J., Sartorius, N., & Maj, M. (2022). Psychiatric diagnosis and treatment in the 21st century: paradigm shifts versus incremental integration. *World Psychiatry: Official Journal of the World Psychiatric Association (WPA), 21*(3), 393–414. https://doi.org/10.1002/wps.20998

Stępnicki, P., Kondej, M., & Kaczor, A. A. (2018). Current concepts and treatments of schizophrenia. *Molecules (Basel, Switzerland), 23*(8), 2087. https://doi.org/10.3390/molecules23082087

Substance Abuse and Mental Health Services Administration. (2014). *Recovery.* National and Regional Resources. https://www.samhsa.gov/sites/default/files/samhsa-recovery-resources_0.pdf

Substance Abuse and Mental Health Services Administration. (2014, September 11). *Recovery services provided by substance abuse treatment facilities in the United States.* https://www.samhsa.gov/data/sites/default/files/NSSATS-SR175-RecoverySvcs-2014/NSSATS-SR175-RecoverySvcs-2014.htm

Substance Abuse and Mental Health Services Administration. (2016). *Impact of the DSM-IV to DSM-5 changes on the National Survey on Drug Use and Health.* CBHSQ Methodology Report. Center for Behavioral Health Statistics and Quality, Substance Abuse and Mental Health Services Administration, Rockville, MD. https://www.ncbi.nlm.nih.gov/books/NBK519697/

Substance Abuse and Mental Health Services Administration. (n.d.). *About recovery.* Substance Use. https://www.samhsa.gov/substance-use/recovery/about

Tadmon, D., & Olfson, M. (2022). Trends in outpatient psychotherapy provision by U.S. psychiatrists: 1996-2016. *The American Journal of Psychiatry, 179*(2), 110–121. https://doi.org/10.1176/appi.ajp.2021.21040338

Téllez-Zenteno, J. F., & Hernández-Ronquillo, L. (2012). A review of the epidemiology of temporal lobe epilepsy. *Epilepsy Research and Treatment, 2012*, 630853. https://doi.org/10.1155/2012/630853

The Baker Center for Children and Families. (2021, July 26). *The Baker Center names Richard Voccio, MBA, as vice president of finance.* Baker Center. https://www.bakercenter.org/news-events/news/judge-baker-childrens-center-names-richard-voccio-mba-as-vice-president-of-finance

The Burke Foundation. (2024). *Adverse childhood experiences (ACESs).* https://burkefoundation.org/what-drives-us/adverse-childhood-experiences-aces/

The U.S. Department of Housing and Urban Development. (2023). *The 2023 annual homelessness assessment report to Congress.* https://www.huduser.gov/portal/sites/default/files/pdf/2023-AHAR-Part-1.pdf

Torrey, E. F., Zdanowicz, M.T. & Kennard, A. D., & Lamb, H. R., Eslinger, D. F., Biasotti, M. C., Fuller, D. A. (2014). *The treatment of persons with mental illness in prisons and jails: A State survey.* Office of Justice Programs. https://www.ojp.gov/ncjrs/virtual-library/abstracts/treatment-persons-mental-illness-prisons-and-jails-state-survey

Treatment Advocacy Center (2012, July 19). *No room at the inn: Trends and consequences of closing public psychiatric hospitals 2005 – 2010.* Treatment Advocacy Center. https://ww1.prweb.com/prfiles/2012/07/18/9703740/No_Room_at_the_Inn-2012.pdf

Treichler, E. B. H., & Spaulding, W. D. (2017). Beyond shared decision-making: Collaboration in the age of recovery from serious mental illness. *The American Journal of Orthopsychiatry, 87*(5), 567–574. https://doi.org/10.1037/ort0000256

Tsabary, S. (2010). *The conscious parent: Transforming ourselves, empowering our children.* Namaste Publishing, Incorporated.

Turkington, D., Lebert, L., & Spencer, H. (2016). Auditory hallucinations in schizophrenia: helping patients to develop effective coping strategies. *BJPsych Advances, 22*(6), 391–396. doi:10.1192/apt.bp.115.015214

Unick, G. J., Bassuk, E. L., Richard, M. K., & Paquette, K. (2019). Organizational trauma-informed care: Associations with individual and agency factors. *Psychological Services, 16*(1), 134–142. https://doi.org/10.1037/ser0000299

Unützer J., Harbin, H., Schoenbaum, M., & Druss, B. (2013). *The collaborative care model: an approach for integrating physical and mental health care in Medicaid Health Homes.* Center for Health Strategies and Mathematica Policy Research.

U.S. Department of Education. (2004). *Individuals with Disabilities Education Act.* Public Law 108–446. https://www.congress.gov/bill/108th-congress/house-bill/1350/text

van den Berg, D., Tolmeijer, E., Jongeneel, A., Staring, A. B. P., Palstra, E., van der Gaag, M., & Hardy, A. (2023). Voice phenomenology as a mirror of the past. *Psychological Medicine, 53*(7), 2954–2962. https://doi.org/10.1017/S0033291721004955

van der Kolk, B. A. (2015). *The body keeps the score: Brain, mind, and body in the healing of trauma.* Penguin Publishing Group.

Van Ysslestyne, J. (2018). *Spirits from the edge of the world: Classical shamanism in Ulchi society.* Pathfinder Counseling.

Wang, E. W. (2019). *The collected schizophrenias: Essays.* Graywolf Press.

Waters, F., & Fernyhough, C. (2017). Hallucinations: A systematic review of points of similarity and difference across diagnostic classes. *Schizophrenia Bulletin, 43*(1), 32–43. https://doi.org/10.1093/schbul/sbw132

Weiner, S. (2022, August 9). *A growing psychiatrist shortage and an enormous demand for mental health.* AAMC News. https://www.aamc.org/news/growing-psychiatrist-shortage-enormous-demand-mental-health-services

Whitaker, R. (2010). *Anatomy of an epidemic: Magic bullets, psychiatric drugs, and the astonishing rise of mental illness in America.* Crown.

Whitebird, R. R., Solberg, L. I., Jaeckels, N. A., Pietruszewski, P. B., Hadzic, S., Unützer, J., Ohnsorg, K. A., Rossom, R. C., Beck, A., Joslyn, K. E., & Rubenstein, L. V. (2014). Effective implementation of collaborative care for depression: what is needed?. *The American Journal of Managed Care*, *20*(9), 699–707.

Woodfox, A. (2019). *Solitary*. Grove Atlantic.

Word Prison Brief. (n.d). *Highest to lowest prison population rate*. Prison Studies. https://www.prisonstudies.org/highest-to-lowest/prison_population_rate?field_region_taxonomy_tid=All

World Health Organization. (2025). *Epilepsy*. Health Topics. https://www.who.int/health-topics/epilepsy#tab=tab_1

Wu, E. Q., Shi, L., Birnbaum, H., Hudson, T., & Kessler, R. (2006). Annual prevalence of diagnosed schizophrenia in the USA: A claims data analysis approach. *Psychological Medicine*, *36*(11), 1535–1540. https://doi.org/10.1017/S0033291706008191

Yanni, C. (2007). *The architecture of madness*. University of Minnesota Press.

Index

aberrant behaviors 62
adolescent behavior 73
adoption 31–2, 34–5
Adverse Childhood Experiences (ACEs) 39–40, 187
aggressive behaviors 38, 57, 60
Alexander II of Russia 18
Amador, Xavier 150
American Psychological Association Committee on Nomenclature and Statistics 87
Angola Prison, Louisiana 137
Anthony, William 157
anti-nausea medicine 80
antipsychotic medications 94
Apocalypse Now 84
Arbour Hospital 123–126
attention deficit-hyperactivity disorder (ADHD) 40, 44, 88, 89, 102
  living with label of 38–9
  overview 37–8
auditory and visual hallucinations 107
autonomy 65, 71, 133, 168, 178

Band, Midnight Oil 109
Basaglia, Franco 133
Bateson, Gregory 142
behavioral dyscontrol 99
Behavioral Health Workforce 136
behavioral management 68
behaviors
  aberrant 62
  aggressive 38, 57, 60
  troubling/unpredictable 83
  unpredictable 62, 80, 83
Being Mortal: Medicine and What Matters in the End (Gawande) 88
Benadryl 94, 127
Berwick, Don 175
Beth Israel Hospital 28–9, 142, 145
Better Homes and Gardens magazine 147
Biden, Joe 190
bipolar and psychotic disorders 99
Bleuler, Eugen 132
Boston State Hospital 26–8
Brooks, Hester 67
Brown, Daniel 67

case managers 3, 80, 161–2, 177, 181–2
Cauley, Michael 67, 68
Center for Psychiatric Rehabilitation (BU) 157–158, 160–1, 163, 182–3
Centers for Medicare and Medicaid Services (CMS) 150
Chapman, Edward 67
Charlton, James 177
childhood trauma 12, 40
Children's Hospital 37, 71
Chlorothiazide 127
chlorpromazine (Thorazine) 134, 170–1
Clozaril (clozapine) 127, 155, 159–60, 171, 179, 182
Coffey, Barbara 46, 67
Cogentin 127
Colbert, Stephen 109
Collaborative Care Model 148–151

community mental health 134, 140, 189
community of spirits 5–16, 105–22
community social activities 67
coping mode 13
Crazy: A Father's Search Through America's Mental Health Madness (Earley) 141
Crossing the Quality Chasm 14
Crowe, Sheryl 109

Dangerfield, Rodney 109
Davidson, Larry 166
Deegan, Patricia 4–5, 133, 172, 188
delusions 94, 96, 102, 124
Department of Education 65
diagnoses 2–4, 87–98, 189
Diagnostic and Statistical Manual of Mental Disorders (DSM) 87–8, 96–7, 106
disabilities 52, 157, 177, 186
disenfranchised grief 12
disruptive behaviors 61
disseminated intravascular coagulopathy (DIC) 28
dissociative disorders 97
dissociative identity disorder (DID) 93
Dix, Dorothea 131–2

Earley, Pete 141
ectopic pregnancy 30
Eikos 102–104, 109, 113, 119
emotional problems 60, 73
"Empowerment Medicine" 172
evaluation procedures 66

family caregivers 130–1
Fay, Sarah 87
Felitti, Vincent J. 39
fires 84, 150–151
First World War 18, 20
fish 79, 84, 156, 167
flat affect 44–5
florid psychosis 123–8
Fogel, Barry 67, 91
Free, appropriate, public education (FAPE) 53
Full Metal Jacket 117

Garrett, Michael 3–4, 143, 184–5
Gawande, Atul 88
Goffman, Erving 14, 133–4
Grief 11–12, 31–2, 40
  disenfranchised 12
  traditional 12
Gymboree program 11

Haldol 127
hallucinations 93–97, 102, 105, 107
  auditory and visual 97, 105, 107
  kinesthetic 97
Hallucinations (Sacks) 95
Hartman, Sergeant 117
Healing: Our Path from Mental Illness to Mental Health (Insel) 87
Hearing Voices Network 120
Herman, Judith 39
herpetologist 80
High Point Hospital 127–128
historical trauma 18, 40
Holocaust 20
homelessness 10, 12, 134, 138, 146
homeschooling program 65, 68–9, 130
hope 157, 183–91
Howe, Irving 18
HUD's Annual Homelessness Assessment Report to Congress 138
Hutchinson, Dori 160–1, 180–2

"impulse disorder NOS" (not otherwise specified) 101–2
Individualized Education Programs (IEPs) 43–4, 53–8, 62, 65–67, 70–1
Individuals with Disabilities Education Act (IDEA) 52–3
Innovation in Behavioral Health Model (IBH) 150
Insel, Thomas 87–8
intergenerational trauma 20, 187

"Is Homelessness a Mental Health Problem?" (Bassuk) 146
is there no place on earth for me? (Sheehan) 146

Jewish 19
Jovel, Albert 66, 177
Jung, Carl 108

Kaiser Permanente 149
Keefe, James 46, 56, 58, 67, 69
Kennedy, John F.
  "bold new approach" 134, 189
  concept of community mental health 134
Keppra 102, 127
Khand, Suruchi 178, 182
kinesthetic hallucinations 97
Kraepelin, Emil 132

Lamictal 85, 91–2, 102, 127
Lifeline Center for Child Development. 23

Mack, John 33, 144
McLean Hospital 69, 99–102
Manville School. 59–62, 65
marginalized children 11–15
Masek, Bruce 67
Massachusetts Comprehensive Assessment System (MCAS) 74
Medicaid 134, 136, 150, 151
Medicare 134, 136, 151
mental health 1–7
  care 27, 59
  residential 62
  system 129–40
mental health system 66, 129–40
mental illness 2–4, 6–7, 130
  effective treatment 27
  interest/knowledge of 85
  perceptions of 14
  and sexism 27
  shame associated with 14
Mental Retardation Facilities and Community Mental Health Centers Construction Act 134
MGH clinical services 161
Montessori Preschool 34, 36–7
Monty Python 86
moral treatment 131–3
My Mysterious Son (Russell) 108

National Center on Family Homelessness 147
National Institute of Mental Health (NIMH) 133
National Mental Health Act 133
Native American 115
neurological illness 59
New Freedom Commission Report 139
"non-system" of care 12

Observations and Inquiries upon the Diseases of the Mind 131
obsessive-compulsive disorder (OCD) 41, 46, 49, 88–91
otherness 11, 14

Pale of Settlement 17–20
Pardes, Herbert 88
parenting 13, 14, 34, 101
Pathological: The true story of six misdiagnoses (Fay) 87
Pathways Academy 69
peer specialists 129, 169, 182
peer workers 129, 157
person-centered 2, 7, 157, 189
Pinel, Philippe 131
polypharmacy 124
Poor Laws 130
post-traumatic stress disorder (PTSD) 40, 92–3, 97
poverty 14, 19, 146
pregnancy 30–1
President's Freedom Commission on Mental Health 139
primary care 148–50
protection and containment policy 68

psychiatric diagnostic system 87
psychiatrist 2, 6, 12, 86, 101, 145
psychiatry. 25, 27, 142
  defined 189
  transforming 141–52
psychoanalysis 27, 143
psychodynamic psychotherapy 27, 144
psychosis 99, 123–128
public mental health institutions 131
purpose 183–91

Quakers 131
The Quiet Room (Schiller) 94

real connection 177–82
real empathy 177–82
real people 177–82
Recovery 4, 5, 165–6, 186–7, 189, 190
Recovery movement 130, 139–40, 143, 174, 190
Recovery-oriented person-centered care 28, 143, 157, 166, 175, 188–9
Recovery process 165–75, 187
  community 168–75
  health 167
  home 166–7
  purpose 167–8
Reed, Aaron 66, 177
rehabilitation crisis 181
residential mental health placement 62
Richmond, Cedric L. 137
Risperdal 127
Rolle, Myron L. 186
Rush, Benjamin 131
Russell, Dick 108

Sacks, Oliver 95, 120
Saks, Elyn 143
Samuda, Jayne 61
Sandler, Adam 109
Schiller, Lori 94–5
schizophrenia 2, 23, 28, 93–8, 105, 106, 132
  described 93–4, 96
  Kraepelinian definition of 4
"Schizophrenogenic mother" 142
The Scimitar 22
Second World War 20
self-esteem 37, 49, 54, 56, 58, 67–8, 74, 81, 85, 99, 156, 162, 168–9, 177, 182, 185
self-image 67
serious mental illness (SMI) 14, 130, 135, 188–9
Seroquel 127
sexism
  in medicine 25
  and mental illness 27
Shatner, William 109
Sheehan, Susan 146
Shonkoff, Jack 39
Side by Side Supported Living (SBS) 129, 158–9, 161–3, 169, 178, 182–3
Simpson, Bart 119
Sloan Kettering Memorial Hospital 24
Snakes 77–79, 155
social communities 80
social conflict resolution strategies 66
socialization 54, 65, 68–9, 71, 180
Solitary (Woodfox) 137–138
South Park television series 113
special education 73
stabbing 61
staffing shortages 136, 137
stigma 14, 98, 186
Substance Abuse and Mental Health Services Administration (SAMHSA) 4, 139, 165–6, 168, 171
substance use disorders (SUD) 151
suicidal behavior 71–73
Swift, Taylor 109
systems issues 13, 186, 188

temporal lobe epilepsy (TLE) 88–9, 91–2
The American Journal of Psychiatry 146
The Better Homes Fund 147
The Center Cannot Hold (Saks) 143
tic disorder 46

tic storms 57, 68
Tikkun Olam 18
Tourette, Gilles de la 89
Tourette Syndrome (TS) 41, 46–7, 51, 60, 73, 84, 88–90
transforming psychiatry 141–52
trauma 142, 146
  and adverse childhood experiences 97
  care protocols 147
  childhood 12, 40
  development of mental illness 92
  and healing 93
  historical 18, 40
  intergenerational 20, 187
Trauma and Recovery (Herman) 39
trauma-informed care 139
traumatic stress 39–40, 184
  and healthcare system 6
Treatment Advocacy Center (TAC) 135–38
treatment team 1, 46, 69, 169, 170, 181, 184
troubling/unpredictable behaviors 83
tzedakah (charity) 18

University of Massachusetts 37
University of Washington AIMS Center 149
unpredictable behavior 62, 80, 83
US Congress 131

Vera Institute of Justice 137
Veterans Administration 149
Voices 97, 107, 108, 115, 119–23, 155, 157–60, 173, 179

Watkins, Virginia 48
Weir, Rachel 149
Wilbur, Donna 161–2, 169, 178, 184, 188
Wild Acres in Lexington, Massachusetts 125
Winthrop House 73–75
Woodfox, Albert 137
World of Our Fathers (Howe) 18

Notes on Authors

Ellen Bassuk, MD, is a pioneering psychiatrist, researcher, clinician, and advocate recognized for her extensive work on mental health, trauma, and homelessness. With a career spanning five decades, Dr. Bassuk has made significant contributions to the understanding and treatment of mental health, particularly in the context of homelessness and vulnerable populations, especially families and children. She began her career training at institutions like Harvard Medical School, where she served as Associate Professor of Psychiatry for almost four decades. Throughout her career, Dr. Bassuk has been deeply committed to both clinical care, program design and service delivery, and social advocacy, founding the National Center on Family Homelessness in 1988, and later C4 Innovations. She has written more than 150 peer-reviewed articles, monographs, and books. An American Psychiatric Association Distinguished Life Fellow, her work has garnered recognition and awards, including an honorary doctorate in public service from Northeastern University, the Blanche F. Ittleson Award for the Promotion of Children's Mental Health, and the American Psychological Association Distinguished Contribution to Child Advocacy Award.

Daniel M. Schoonover is a passionate animal lover and dedicated volunteer with a deep commitment to the well-being of often-forgotten or ignored creatures and communities. With a diverse background in animal care, including hands-on experience in herpetology and marine life management, he has devoted much of his life to nurturing the natural world, including volunteering at the Woods Hole Science Aquarium to caring for animals at the MSPCA. Currently enrolled in the BU Center for Psychiatric Rehabilitation, Daniel is expanding his knowledge in spirituality, recovery, and wellness, while continuing to deepen his understanding of herpetology through the Amphibian Foundation's program. He is currently volunteering as a gardner at a church in Brookline and working at a food bank. Whether tending to animals, assisting those in need, or exploring new pathways in personal development, he is committed to making a meaningful impact in the world around him.